EStars
Classroom of the Future

David Kerrigan

With a foreword by Dr. Terence P. Brady,
Curriculum Development Director, Misk Foundation

EStars Classroom of the Future (ESCotF)

This book was written to coincide with the unveiling of
the EStars Classroom of the Future
at the Misk Global Forum November 2023
in association with Riyadh Schools Platform, Saudi Arabia

Features specific to the version of the room displayed at
the event are highlighted as 'ESCotF@MGF'

For the latest details, please visit https://estars.pro/escotf

Foreword

I wonder what the 'classroom' will look like in the future as we move through the fourth industrial revolution and into the fifth?

What will it be for? What will it aim to achieve? Will all students and not just high performers thrive in this classroom? Will its very purpose be different?

I wonder!

The Greek philosopher Plato is credited with saying that all philosophy or ideas begin with 'wonder'. In his dialogue Theaetetus, Socrates says to his student, "*I see, my dear Theaetetus, that Theodorus had a true insight into your nature when he said that you were a philosopher; for wonder is the feeling of a philosopher, and philosophy begins in wonder.*" (Plato, Theaetetus 155c-d, tr.)

Aristotle also emphasized the importance of wonder in the pursuit of knowledge. In his book Metaphysics, he writes, "*It is through wonder that people both now and at first began to philosophize, wondering originally about the obvious difficulties, and then advancing by degrees to greater matters.*" (Aristotle. Aristotle in 23 Volumes, Vols.17, 18, translated by Hugh Tredennick. Cambridge, MA, Harvard University Press; London, William Heinemann Ltd. 1933, 1989)

In other words, both Plato and Aristotle believed that philosophy, ideas, thinking, pondering and musing begin with a sense of wonder about the world around us.

First and foremost, the EStars Classroom of the Future will be a place of 'wonder'.

When we wonder about things, we are motivated to learn more. This curiosity leads 'all' to ask questions, to research, to develop new thinking, to be innovative, to be active rather than passive and ultimately to embrace and thrive in the ambiguity and uncertainty of the future.

The importance of wonder in education is recognized as highly important. Many philosophers and educationalists believe that wonder is essential for critical thinking and creativity. It allows us to challenge assumptions, question the educational status quo, and explore new possibilities.

Ever since I read about the innovative futuristic cities like NEOM and Misk City etc., my educational mind began to wonder and question.

I began asking questions like: What will the future classroom look like in these cities? How will classrooms in these cities change in the future? What new technologies and teaching methods will be used in classrooms in these cities in the future? What will be the role of the teacher in the future classroom in these cities? How will classrooms in these cities be designed to support student learning in the future?

From Wonder to Action

Delivering the best possible learning opportunities to our students is always our north star. We never settle, and we constantly look for ways to not just keep up, but to forge ahead. Building on the pioneering work we've done, we're ready to wonder what's next; the classroom of the future.

Everything we do at the Riyadh Schools Platform is set within the context of Saudi Arabia's Vision 2030, the ambitious and far-reaching national transformation plan to diversify the Kingdom's economy in support of sustainable, long-term economic and social success. This blueprint, which has been designed to elevate the nation to new horizons, places education at its very heart, recognising its role as the cornerstone for a prosperous and sustainable future. But the world of 2030 and beyond that our pupils will graduate into is a world unlike what's gone before. What wonderful ambiguity and uncertainty. Our graduates need to be prepared for these new but wonderful challenges in new ways.

Challenging Change

The Classroom of the Future must be a learning space to better equip students to navigate this evolving landscape, and these trends form the basis of our project scope:

Disruptive Technologies: The pace at which technology is evolving is unprecedented. By 2030, we can expect to see further advancements in artificial intelligence, biotechnology, quantum computing, and more. Our educational system must equip students with the skills to navigate, utilise, and even pioneer these technologies.

Changing Job Market: Many of the jobs that exist today will have changed radically by 2030. Just read the Future Jobs Report, the research is clear. New professions will emerge that we haven't even conceived of yet. To ensure our children are not only employable but also innovators in their fields, we must provide them with adaptable core skills, global competences and a growth mindset to wonder.

Global Challenges: Issues such as climate change, global health crises, and geopolitical tensions require a new generation of thinkers who are collaborative, critical, and solution-oriented. Updated teaching methods can emphasise these skills and the importance of global citizenship, while sustainability must be integrated into the classroom.

Diverse Learning Needs: As we learn more about the spectrum of human cognition, it's clear that one-size-fits-all teaching doesn't cater to all students. A full range of learners need to be catered for and we must design curricula to meet the needs of ALL students. Modern teaching methods are more inclusive and personalised, ensuring all students have an equitable chance at success. Traditional teaching methods, while foundational, may not resonate with the digital-native generation. By integrating modern tools and methods, education remains relevant, engaging, and effective for all students.

Emphasis on Soft Skills: While hard skills are vital, soft skills like empathy, collaboration, communication, calm mindedness and emotional intelligence will be equally crucial in a globally connected world. Modern teaching methods incorporate these skills as core components of the curriculum.

Shift from Memorisation to Application: The internet has made information readily accessible. The value isn't just in knowing facts but understanding concepts and applying knowledge in real-world contexts. Updated teaching methods emphasise experiential learning, critical thinking, and problem-solving.

Promotion of Lifelong Learning: The future will demand continuous learning and adaptability. New teaching methods instil a love for learning and teach students how to learn, to becoming an autodidact, ensuring they can acquire new skills and knowledge throughout their lives.

Mental and Emotional Well-being: Modern educational approaches recognize the importance of students' mental and emotional well-being, integrating mindfulness, resilience, and support structures into the learning process.

Cultural and Social Evolution: As societies evolve, so do their values, cultures, and social norms. Education must reflect these changes to foster acceptance, inclusivity, and a broader understanding of diverse perspectives.

Ethical Considerations of New Technologies: With the rise of technologies like AI and biotech, ethical dilemmas will become increasingly complex. It's crucial to teach students not just how to use technology, but also to consider its societal implications.

The bottom line is that the world of 2030 and beyond will be markedly different from today's landscape and today's education techniques need to evolve too. By updating our teaching methods, we ensure that our children are not just passive participants in this future, but active shapers of it. They deserve an education that prepares them for the challenges and opportunities that await, and we hold the responsibility to provide it.

The Team and the Technology

At the heart of this transformative journey for our students are teachers and parents. Their roles, far from being diminished in this tech-augmented landscape, become even more crucial. Teachers, with their wisdom and experience, guide students through uncharted waters, ensuring that amidst the digital whirlwind, the core values of critical thinking, empathy, and creativity are never lost. Our teachers are a crucial part in realising our vision for the future. As a school, we strive to equip them with the tools that will empower them to unlock each child's maximum potential. We also deeply value the role of parents in education. Parents, the pillars of support, work in tandem with educators, ensuring that the home and school environment act in synergy.

As we traverse this exciting frontier, it's paramount to remember that the essence of education is not solely tethered to the innovations we see or the technology we acquire. Instead, it's about how we pragmatically apply these tools to foster an environment that nurtures minds, cultivates talent, and prepares our youth for the challenges and opportunities of tomorrow. Technology, in all its grandeur, is but an instrument—a means to an end. The true value lies in how we use it to bridge gaps, enhance learning, and create experiences that resonate on a deeply human level.

Delivering a new, future-ready curriculum needs a learning space to match the ambition. The classroom of the future is a facilitator and a catalyst of ambition. We firmly believe in grounding our ambition in best practices, academic rigour and tackling real, meaningful outcomes.

Partnering for Success

Building the best classroom of the future is a profound undertaking, and one that needs experts and thought leaders but also pragmatists who can deliver. That's why we turned to EStars as our partners to join us in our wonder about the classroom of the future. As the global leaders in next-generation esports learning, they share our passion to be at the cutting edge of education that's relevant, energises student curiosity, ignites new passions and enhances skill sets. But they also understand the need to plot a path to the future that starts today.

As we worked with EStars, they brought a clarity of thinking, practical attitude and commitment to the learning sciences that aligned perfectly with our vision. We are proud of what we've achieved together. In this era of rapid advancements and transformative change, the Classroom of the Future emerges as a timely exploration into the evolving landscape of education, particularly within the context of Saudi Arabia's ambitious Vision2030.

In essence, building a classroom of the future is not about chasing the latest gadgets but about creating an environment that holistically nurtures the next generation. It's an investment in a future where our students are empowered, enlightened, and equipped to shape the world positively. The Classroom of the Future is about advancing education; working with EStars, we've focused on bringing to life a harmonious blend of people and technology. It's about understanding that our greatest asset is our human potential, and technology, when used thoughtfully, can amplify this potential manifold.

As you delve into the pages of this book, I hope you find inspiration in the possibilities that lie ahead and recognize the collective responsibility we hold in shaping an educational framework that aligns with Vision2030. A vision that is not just about economic growth, but the growth of minds, spirits, and dreams. Welcome to the wonderful future of education—a future we're excited to embrace.

Terence

Dr. Terence P Brady

Curriculum Development Director,
Riyadh Schools Platform, Misk Foundation

CONTENTS

Table of Contents

Chapter 1: The Education Imperative *1*

The EStars Approach 2

Meet The EStars Classroom of the Future Concept 4

Chapter 2: The Education Ambition *9*

Changing Education 9

Classrooms Reimagined 11

ESCotF Rationale 12

The Role of (Appropriate) Technology 13

Faster Horses and the next Industrial Revolution 15

Learning Aspirations 17

Part 1: Physical Space *21*

The Third Teacher 21

Architecture and Education 22

Size Matters 25

The Classroom Environment Impact 26

Beyond the Architecture: Classroom Design & Indoor Environment
Quality (IEQ) 29

Air Quality & Temperature 29

ESCotF and Indoor Environment Quality (IEQ) 30

Airborne Pollutants 31

Health Benefits 34

Lighting 36

Lighting and well-being 37

Shining a Light on Education 38

Brighter Students 39

Natural Light 40
Artificial Light...41
Lighting Controls...43
Visual Comfort 44
ESCotF Active Lighting: Flexibility & Integrations 45
In Camera...45

Acoustics **46**
Listen & Learn 46
Sound Matters 47
Impacts of Poor Acoustics 49
Sound Design 51
Teacher Benefits...52
ESCotF Sound..53

Layout, Furniture, Fittings & Equipment (FF&E)....................**54**
The Importance of Seating 54
Flexibility For The Win 55
Devices..57
Decorations...57
Distractions...59
Positive Stimuli 60

The Immersive ESCotF@MGF Room **62**

Sustainability & the Environment.......................................**62**

Building the ESCotF **63**

Part 2: Teaching Methods...**67**

Know Your Audience...**68**

Beneficial Buzzwords **69**
Failing to Teach...70

The Need for New Pedagogies **71**
Complex Curricula - An OECD perspective............................72
The Seven Principles of Learning 74
Pedagogies in Practice 75

The Key Teaching Trends...**76**

Active Learning **78**

Modernising Assessments 80

The Role of Technology in Pedagogy **82**

The Future is Flipped **83**

Flipped vs Traditional...85

X-Based Learning **85**

Challenge Based Learning (CBL)..86

Inquiry Based Learning (IBL) 88

PBL...91

Computational Thinking 93

Kinesthetics/Learning by Doing 94

Gaming **94**

Metacognition **97**

Teachers of the Future **100**

Teach Better, Not Harder **101**

The Super-Teacher **102**

Universal Design for Learning (UDL) **104**

The Role of AI in Teaching **106**

Part 3: Lessons For The Future *107*

A Moving Target **107**

Tradition & Well-being 108

Teaching Targets...108

Skills for the Future **110**

Next Industrial Revolution Subjects **111**

Technology Showcase **111**

Virtual Reality (VR) Zone..112

Robotics Zone 119

3D-MakerZone...125

Holography 129

Tech for Teachers 134

Part 4: Room Layouts..**135**

Virtual Floorplans with Lightguides 135

Direct Teaching - Stage...136

Direct Teaching - Hologram 138

Games Mode 140

Group Collaboration Mode 142

Nature Mode 144

Zones Mode 146

Conclusion **149**

The Future is a Journey 149

What's Past is Prologue 151

References..**155**

Chapter 1: The Education Imperative

The classrooms of the past are not fit for the future. Our approach to education needs to be overhauled to reflect the rapidly changing world our children will inhabit. The EStars Classroom of the Future (EScotF) is an ambitious project to reimagine education for the next generation. It will combine the latest thinking in cognitive psychology, the new skills required for the future and the appropriate use of advanced technologies to create a world-leading education experience that starts to make a difference today.

EStars has designed a concept Classroom of the Future where we can unlock the full potential of future generations. We believe that the education spaces of the future should reflect the changed and changing realities of what our education systems must deliver. The time children spend in classrooms during their formative years is precious and we have an obligation to optimise this time, to continuously improve both the physical environment and the teaching and learning activities that take place in our schools.

The era of static, knowledge-heavy curricula is over. What we now teach needs to be dynamic, modern and relevant; it needs to be adaptive and engaging. We need to look beyond outdated modes of assessment and focus on learning outcomes that genuinely prepare students for life, equipping them to succeed in uncertain times.

The teachers of the future will become educators in the true meaning of the word - not just instructors and administrators, but motivators, mentors and coaches. The EScotF gives teachers an array of new tools to amplify their impact on improving learning outcomes.

The careers of the future require new subjects and skills that align with increasingly technology-infused workplaces. AI, robotics, biotech, materials, quantum and metaverse technologies will change the human experience to an unprecedented extent in the next decades. Harnessing these technologies requires us to reset our approach to education and acknowledge the urgency of reform.

According to UNICEF[1], less than half of young people around the world are currently on track to acquire the full range of skills needed to thrive at work and in life.

It is imperative that we challenge ourselves today to invest in developing childrens' creativity and capabilities for a world reshaped by exponential change. We must equip our teachers to unlock the potential of each student, using the very best teaching methods and technologies available. We must extend curricula to include soft skills and emerging technologies. Yet we must not lose sight of the importance of nature in our automated future. Thus, we've built our room to incorporate a vertical farm and we constantly monitor 9 aspects of air quality. From mental and physical well-being to environmental influences, our education ambition must embrace culture, sustainability and humanity.

Education no longer has to be one-size-fits-all. We can realistically aspire to provide our children with fully personalised learning built on proven cognitive psychology principles and realised through a combination of human ingenuity and technological capability. By adapting our classrooms to embrace the best of nature, pedagogical tradition and cutting-edge immersive technologies, the conceptual classroom of the future has arrived. Let's build it today.

The EStars Approach

The impact of the project to imagine the evolution of the classroom will be profound. Every improvement we identify can change lives for the better. Each positive adjustment can move a generation - and nation - forwards.

As a starting point, we have analysed the great work of numerous educational researchers across the globe. We have explored the research that often goes un-implemented in the pressures of day-to-day schooling, to find the data-driven improvements that will make a difference - starting now. We sought to dislodge inertia by revisiting the prevailing assumptions around where, how and what we teach, along with the why.

We wanted our thinking to be open and expansive - questioning the status quo yet respecting proven traditions. We wanted our proposals to be ambitious but pragmatic - experimental but rooted in evidence-based methods. We wanted to inspire debate about a future state, while starting to build now with today's technologies.

As we set about designing the classroom of the future, we had identified three broad areas we wanted to address in the quest for improved, fit-for-the-future teaching and learning outcomes that could genuinely enhance education:

- the physical space,
- the approach to teaching (pedagogy) and
- the topics & technologies (subject matter)

And we wanted to tackle these three areas sustainably. Building the Classroom of the Future should be an iterative process. There are some quick wins, but a truly modern education system will continuously adapt through constant improvement, regularly reassessing the alignment between objectives and outcomes, industrial relevance and technological advances.

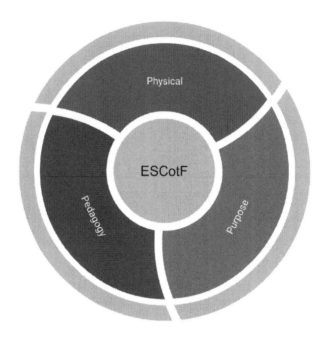

Figure: The EStars Classroom of the Future Circle of Influences

Although superficially quite simple, a classroom is in fact a complex interplay of factors, physical, psychological and technological. Even within those topics, there are myriad sub-factors contributing to the overall results - a veritable 'wicked'[12] problem. But there are few greater ambitions than advancing our children's education and preparing them as best we can to create the future. Building the best classrooms we can is a privilege and a priority.

Meet The EStars Classroom of the Future Concept

The EStars Classroom of the Future (ESCotF) doesn't look like any classroom you've seen before. It's a unique concept that breaks new ground in delivering a space, across multiple domains, for teaching and learning. We've reimagined the classroom as a flexible resource that's adaptable by design. It's conceived to be engaging, interactive and responsive. It's inclusive, accessible and technologically advanced, yet fundamentally *human*.

A classroom should facilitate learning, not dictate the pedagogy. So, ESCotF is not just a single room. It's able to morph into different environments to create a learning experience that's optimised for each student and each subject. For a history lesson, it can transform into an ancient village; for esports, it can be an exhilarating tournament venue; for STEM it can be a robot factory and for well-being, it can be a relaxing forest-scape. For group collaborations, it can be arranged into zones, while the innovative pods can be arranged in an infinite range of seating layouts.

The ESCotF relies on flexible design and appropriate digital technology to empower teachers to engage with children as never before. We will break the traditional fourth wall of Victorian-era classrooms to appeal to the students' senses (literally - there are scent dispensers in the room!), capture their attention and scaffold their development for a truly next-generation learning experience. The focus is on enabling the skills that the world of 2030 and beyond will need, not the rigid education structures inherited from the last century.

The EStars Classroom of the Future project is designed to reimagine education, but it is not an exercise in innovation theatre. Although we're exploring future possibilities, we're also identifying improvements that can be harnessed in the short term. Our design prioritises evidence-based advances in the physical characteristics of the room, modern teaching methods and future-relevant skills. As mentioned above, we have questioned the where (room design), how (pedagogy) and what (skills) that education for the future needs to redefine.

In Part 1, we'll examine the influence of the physical space, emphasising its ability to facilitate optimal learning of future-relevant knowledge and skills in an instructionally-sound way. Research has shown the importance of the physical aspects of a room in learning outcomes, so we've focused on air quality, lighting, acoustics and visual stimulation. One study found that optimising all of these physical characteristics of primary classrooms improved academic performance in reading, writing, and mathematics by 16 percent[3].

We've created the room to be child-centric but teacher-empowered. From a teaching perspective, we've combed the research to extract the best new and proven methods, but gone further to turn them from aspirational buzzwords into pragmatic tools that represent progress, not just change. As we'll discuss in Part 2, among the domains we're leveraging are:

- UDL (Universal Design for Learning)
- Pedagogy/Andragogy/Heutagogy
- Flipped Classroom
- Active Learning
- Cognitive Psychology
- Metacognition
- Desirable Difficulties
- Challenge Based Learning
- Multiple Intelligence Theory
- Formal to Informal Learning

As children develop, research shows that somewhere between age 12 and 15, most children start to exhibit adult learning characteristics, where curiosity is more important than curriculum. Historically, we have continued to teach them using rigid methods that are not attuned to this insight. As they move from responding better to adult-centric andragogy than child-centric pedagogy, our room offers tactile and interactive learning that aligns with the demands of Industry, just as our esports configuration unlocks the myriad educational benefits of gaming.

Part 3 describes how we have equipped the classroom of the future with active learning technologies that students can master, enabling them to acquire the skills they'll need in the workplaces of the future, as well as the competencies future employers seek.

Our room is designed with 4 guiding principles. We start with the latest breakthroughs in teaching and cognitive psychology. We augment the learning journey with the latest immersive and interactive technologies that are proven to enhance engagement. We celebrate the importance of nature, well-being and sustainability. And our remarkably flexible room can be reconfigured in an instant to excel across disciplines - from history and art to science and gaming. From Theory and Soft Skills to practical exercises, we believe in inclusivity and creating a sense of exploration.

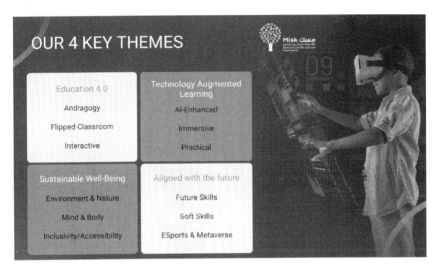

Figure: The 4 key themes of the EStars Classroom of the Future

Ultimately, everything we do is motivated by a commitment to improved outcomes for students. It requires a concerted collaborative effort from curriculum designers, teachers, parents, schools and students, supported by technologists, architects, industry leaders and policy makers.

There are few higher callings than investing in our children. Remember, a classroom is so much more than a room: it is literally where we create the future. It is where we unlock the potential of future generations, and where we must equip our children to shape their nation.

Chapter 2: The Education Ambition

Humanity has a long history of educating. As with many things from ancient times, it's hard to be sure exactly when the first schools were established. According to some scholars, that honour belongs to Egypt and Sumeria: the first formal education began shortly after the development of writing (c. 3000 BCE), when both the Sumerians (who had developed a cuneiform system of picto-graphics) and the Egyptians (who developed hieroglyphics) established schools to teach students to read and write the systems. The first school that was open to everyone, not just the upper classes, may well have been that established by Chinese philosopher Confucius (551–479 BCE), who taught literature and music, conduct, and ethics to anyone who wanted to learn, while modern systems stem from the ancient Greek schools, which were founded about the fifth century BCE.[4]

For all the history and progress of education over the centuries, we've reached a point where our current approach is struggling to match the reality of what lies ahead. Ivan Illich's work[5] warned of the dangers of a system out of touch with what matters: *"The pupil is thereby "schooled" to confuse teaching with learning, grade advancement with education, a diploma with competence, and fluency with the ability to say something new"*. We must now be visionary enough to recognise that today's processes are no longer aligned with emerging realities and change is imperative.

Changing Education

Education 4.0 is a term sometimes used to describe the new approach to learning that is aligned with the emerging needs of high-tech work (often referred to as the 4th or 5th Industrial Revolution). As we'll discuss in the upcoming sections, we envisage changes across virtually all elements of education - what is taught, how it's taught, how it's assessed and the role of technology in supporting learning.

Making drastic changes in education is not easy. Rightly, there is a concern about moving too fast and accepting unproven hyperbolic claims about new technologies or pedagogies. In the absence of something demonstrably better than current best practices, together with the short-term costs of changes at national scale, as well as a lack of time/resources, many previous attempts at reform have stalled.

"We'd rather our kids went through the flawed system that we ourselves survived than submit them to something untested and unknown".[6]

Justin Reich, Director of the MIT Teaching Systems Lab

The hesitancy to change is understandable. The Silicon Valley style of innovation to "Move Fast and Break things" isn't appropriate in education. We face the somewhat contradictory imperative to offer every child the best we have (i.e., the proven approach) vs what we *think* might be better.

The focus on frequent examination cycles often precludes anything vaguely experimental. Ahead of meaningful change comes the need to challenge the accepted wisdom that a good examination grade is a reliable proxy for success in later life and an appropriate assessment of cumulative educational attainment across anything but 'hard' skills. And of course, we have a duty not to disadvantage children by trialling something that may ultimately not prove to be as effective as current best practice, a concept we'll explore more in Part 2.

But, in the face of massive disruptive forces and obvious impending AI and automation-induced tumult in numerous industries, we cannot afford to be overly cautious. We must be pragmatic but ambitious. That's why EStars has an emphasis on getting the foundational elements right, before layering on new methods and technologies. We've kept teachers and students at the heart of our thinking, recognising the role of technology as a means, not an end. Achieving sustainable, effective change requires a truly holistic approach that considers the interplay of all stakeholders and influences.

Classrooms Reimagined

Classrooms are among the most important rooms in our world. The physical and digital spaces where education takes place have lifelong impacts on our children. We know our children will grow up in a very different world, a world shaped by AI and exponential technologies, a world that will require new skills. We also know that you can't effectively teach the skills of the future in the classrooms of the past.

It seems sensible to scrutinise the suitability and efficacy of the rooms and practices we entrust our children to for 6 or 7 hours a day. But in a time of rapid technological advances and shifting target outcomes, we must recalibrate with more urgency and a willingness to embrace fundamental change.

Although there is clearly educational merit in classroom settings, there is also something contrived and limiting about them, frequently rendering them unrepresentative of the world at large, especially the workplaces that students will transition into. Our emphasis on flexibility in the ESCotF is borne of a recognition that, as students mature, we must introduce autonomy into their learning experience, giving them room (and permission) to explore learning rather than just receive knowledge.

Classrooms need to evolve from closed, impenetrable, inward-looking spaces focused on success measured only in exam grades. Instead, they must actively look outwards to satisfy future trends and align with their true purpose - providing holistic education that goes beyond standardised testing to include the digital, social and vocational skills the future demands. Before we dive too deeply into technology-led solutions, then, we should consider the physical changes that can augment and amplify the undoubtedly huge changes that software and technology will bring in the years ahead.

ESCotF Rationale

ESCotF is built to deliver engagement and improved results, not tick boxes or maintain the status quo. ESCotF is about delivering modern, holistic learning solutions that make a real difference. It straddles the present and the future; built on the solid foundation of the past, but ready to move beyond the technological and pedagogical constraints of the last two decades. ESCotF brings together EStars' deep technological expertise with our commitment to the human side of learning. We know that effective learning is about learner experience, cognitive psychology and personal growth, not just the traditional scope of historic and contemporary schools.

Smarter teaching solutions designed even 20 years ago have served us well. But they haven't kept up with the increasingly complex needs of today's environment. They were designed for a different era - the context has changed (more emphasis on skills, competencies and just-in-time learning) and so too has the content (more bite sized learning, more video and interactive content) while the enabling technological landscape has changed drastically (mobile, AI, XR).

The purpose of classrooms hasn't changed - they should be a space to let children learn. Crucially though, the future that classrooms are preparing kids for is changing. We set out to create a classroom that disrupts the incumbent model of learning. Not for the sake of disruption, but to better prepare for the future. It will come to life as students explore, grow and push the boundaries of what is possible in a classroom.

Pedagogy is at the heart of teaching and learning. Preparing young people to meet new challenges means a reappraisal and update of the pedagogies teachers use now. We strongly believe in the central role that the learning sciences should play in designing the classrooms of the future. Drawing on the work of leading researchers in the space[7], we have infused our plans with an eye on learning, not just teaching. The ESCotF is like a toolkit - we want to empower teachers to deliver better outcomes for students. We're not determining what will happen within the room - we believe that is best left to the educators - but we want to expand what's possible.

In this project, we're imagining the ingredients for the classroom of the future but driving the conversation with the technologies of the present. We've set out to build both a practical working classroom for today and a path to tomorrow. Even absent any further dramatic technical breakthroughs, we can extrapolate the substantial and significant developments to come in the field of technology-enhanced learning and imagine how they will evolve and proliferate in the years ahead. Some of the technology we talk about here is available today, though perhaps not yet affordable. But technology always gets cheaper, so it's safe to assume devices that are out of mainstream reach today won't be for long.

The Role of (Appropriate) Technology

"I don't think that technologies, per se, are going to change classrooms if they're not addressing the deep level of learning. If it's just superficial and if it's just having some digital device in front of you but actually doing the exact same thing as doing without this device, then it's not changing anything."[8]

Dr Hanna Dumont, Educational Psychologist

The role of technology in education has proven controversial in the past. Projects that <u>impose</u> technology on classrooms are unlikely to succeed. Hence, we focus on which technologies can add meaningful new learning experiences to better engage students and elicit more modern or improved learning outcomes. We know that our efforts to insert technology into teaching must be done only with clear purpose - without accompanying supporting systemic change, we risk teaching the same old materials with a digital veneer.

Leading education entrepreneur Sal Khan warns of the need for "the enlightened use of technology. It's natural for any of us with engineering backgrounds or technology backgrounds to get enamoured with the technology, and then look for a problem to solve with that, and I think that usually does not work out so well. You should always first say, 'What are you trying to solve?' And then don't immediately gravitate to the fanciest way to solve it."[9]

Technology should be used to support - not define - learning. Learning technology should be rooted in modern learning theory, and able to meet the diverse needs of contemporary learners, organisations and IT administrators.

Classrooms must be more than mere content distribution places and become truly learning spaces aligned with the future. They must adapt to their users, embrace appropriate emerging technologies and deliver meaningful results. In short, they must become true Classrooms of the Future.

As we think about the appropriate use of technology in the classroom of the future (and indeed, in the classrooms of the present), there is some very informative research to factor into how technology and, in particular, screens and video materials can be best used. The book E-Learning and the Science of Instruction[10] cautions against overly complex mixtures of media which can result in cognitive overload and dissonance, while neuroscientist Maryanne Wolf[11], coined the term "biliterate brain," when researching the relative merits of screen- and page-based reading. A 2019 meta-analysis[12] showed that students understood more informational text when they read on paper compared to on tablets. These findings suggest we must be careful not to over-use the powerful audio-visual technologies at our disposal, nor should we totally abandon paper-based reading.

There are, of course, important wider issues around the role of technology in education and in broader society. The ESCotF team is mindful of concerns around screentime, inappropriate online content and the sustainability of the devices supply chain. Although these are largely outside the scope of this project, we acknowledge their importance in creating a comprehensive strategy for the future.

Faster Horses and the next Industrial Revolution

Perhaps the biggest driver of change in education is the realisation that the learnings students leave school with today aren't sufficient for the future.

Much of the existing work to develop education feels like it has taken a 'faster horses' approach; doing more of the same rather than jumping to a new paradigm. This is the thinking made famous by Henry Ford when he said that "If I had asked my customers what they wanted they would have said a faster horse."

The message from industry is already clear - they're concerned about the gap between good exam grades and the real skills required in the modern workplace, a gap they fear is extending. It's time for an urgent re-examination of the skills, competencies and knowledge learners will require to function successfully in the workplace and in building a modern society.

The UN signposted this need in the 2016 Sustainable Development Goals, with Sustainable Development Goal 4[13] calling for skills beyond traditional literacy and numeracy. This means that education systems will need to adapt their curricula, pedagogies and assessment systems to ensure that students are empowered to develop the skills of the future.

Defining the skills that will be of value in the future is not easy. Vague terms like '21st century skills' and 'fourth industrial revolution' are frequently mentioned across both academic and public discourses but do not always have a common meaning. What is clear, though, is that the role of technology in the future workplace and our relationship with it are changing on a revolutionary scale.

A research collaboration between Microsoft and McKinsey in 2018[14] highlighted that "our education system needs to prepare students for the future in a very different way than it has in the past....new thinking and practices are needed to ensure students develop both the cognitive and social-emotional skills necessary to succeed in their personal and professional lives. While the class of 2030 will need deeper cognitive skills in priority areas such as creativity and problem solving, social-emotional skills such as relationship building, self-awareness, and self-recognition will be increasingly important, since they not only support academic learning but also promote well-being.

The strongest signal from the study was the need for teachers, schools, and school leaders to help students develop stronger social-emotional skills. While not new in education, these skills are newly important. They are taking centre stage alongside cognitive skills and content knowledge in the classroom and in the workforce. Research has found that high-level social-emotional skills developed during childhood are correlated with a number of beneficial long-term health and well-being outcomes as adults, including lower rates of obesity, substance abuse and criminal activity, as well as greater satisfaction in relationships and positive contributions to society.

According to The International Society for Technology in Education (ISTE) there are seven main skills that learners should master:[15]

1. Empowered Learners
2. Digital Citizens
3. Knowledge Constructors
4. Innovative Designers
5. Computational Thinkers
6. Creative Communicators
7. Global Collaborators

This is a useful guiding framework, though will need to be adapted, and perhaps extended, locally. Educators will have to ensure that both the teachers and the facilities in schools are flexible enough and supported with sufficient investment, to accommodate this shift in emphasis.

Andreas Schleicher, OECD Education Directorate described the changing world of education[16]:

"Education today is much more about ways of thinking which involve creative and critical approaches to problem-solving and decision-making. It is also about ways of working, including communication and collaboration, as well as the tools they require, such as the capacity to recognise and exploit the potential of new technologies, or indeed, to avert their risks. And last but not least, education is about the capacity to live in a multi-faceted world as an active and engaged citizen." He also highlights the need for a more cross-disciplinary approach and defines 21st century literacy as about reading to learn and developing the capacity and motivation to identify, understand, interpret, create and communicate knowledge. Success, he says, will go to those individuals and countries that are swift to adapt, slow to resist and open to change.

Learning Aspirations

"Children learn best when intrinsically motivated. They are motivated when respected, encouraged, and exposed to opportunities that capture their interest, build on their previous experience. Children are naturally born learners. They are motivated and are able to learn on their own, given the opportunities and materials. In fact, research suggests that children learn more effectively without being directly or explicitly instructed. They learn from their peers through collaborative learning. They learn by doing through authentic project-based learning. They construct knowledge, test hypotheses, and formulate new ideas through exploring and experimenting socially and individually"[17].

Learning should be about more than just acquiring a certain body of knowledge or set of skills; it includes the growth of the whole person. As we created the ESCotF, among other sources, we drew on the ethos of the Riyadh Schools Platform (see table below) as a guiding principle for our design choices. The ESCotF is the perfect environment to mould the students of the future to be:

- A successful learner, ready to embrace challenges.
- A confident individual, grounded in Saudi values yet open to the world.
- A responsible citizen, cherishing the past and sculpting the future.
- A prepared global citizen, bridging local nuances with global demands.

Strong Sense of Self	Self-directed learning Self-evaluative skills Moderate, tolerant, adaptable and flexible Holistic understanding of well-being Accountability
Prepared	Skill-driven approach, Innovative Mindset Mastery in applying new learning Problem-solving with ideative solutions Critical and reflective thinking Experienced in AI & AR technologies
Ready for the Future	Adaptable nature, Goal-focused Values all learning experiences Contributor to sustainability and economic growth Globally competitive mindset Collaborative spirit
Love of Learning & Application	Strong intellectual foundation with mastery in core subjects Proficiency in bilingual communication A valued contributor to local society Entrepreneurial spirit with global competencies Proactive in environmental initiatives
Highly Motivated	Driven by intrinsic values Radiates self-confidence and high self-esteem Embraces a servant leadership approach, with entrepreneurial instincts Finds joy in learning and its real-world application Fearlessly explores new horizons with a growth mindset Aspires for continuous growth and excellence

International Context

Globally, there is growing emphasis on how education systems need to be reimagined. For example, a 2022 European Commission study[18] noted that "Not being smart, effective, or inclusive in educational infrastructure investments is not just a waste of precious resources, but more importantly a missed educational and cultural opportunity." The report also highlighted the need for improved physical learning environments that were accessible, optimal for learning, safe & healthy and sustainable, all of which apply to the ESCotF.

Part 1: Physical Space

"bad school houses are silent killers of teaching and student learning"

C. Kenneth Tanner[19]

Much of the global future-focused education commentary to date has revolved around changes to the subjects being taught, or the adoption of technology in the classroom. And while we'll move on to tackle these topics, our project starts with a review of some of the physical attributes of the classroom of the future - characteristics that can significantly influence the efficacy of the teaching and technology approaches that are chosen to be deployed within the learning space itself.

The impact of physical classroom design on learning outcomes and its ability to amplify other efforts to improve education has been somewhat neglected, though some insightful research has been carried out that offers evidence and valuable guidance for policy makers. The pandemic sharpened focus on the role of online learning which, of course, will continue to play an important part in the future of learning, but we shouldn't overlook the opportunities we still have to improve classroom-based learning. We need to examine the influence of the physical space and its ability to facilitate optimal learning of more future-focused knowledge and competencies.

The Third Teacher

"There are three teachers of children: adults, other children, and their physical environment."

Loris Malaguzzi

A school project in Italy (the Reggio Emilia Approach) has famously explored the concept of the classroom environment as an important factor in education - acting as the third teacher, alongside the adult teacher and peer learning.

Creating the best environment for teaching is a key contributor to the success of the education process and requires intentionally and purposefully designing the learning environment. The goal of classroom design should be to create an environment that inspires curiosity, encourages collaboration, facilitates active learning and adapts easily to different needs.

Some designers regard classrooms as just a backdrop – but we think of the ESCotF as an active contributor to the learning process, not just a passive, inanimate object. And drawing on the work of Urie Bronfenbrenner and his ecological systems theory, it's important to consider the holistic interplay between the school and wider systems/stakeholders - so we recommend involving parents, policy makers and industry in optimising the physical environment, as well as the curriculum and pedagogy. As Henry Sanoff[20] also put it: *Participatory design, a significant part of quality based on ownership of the plan, recognizes that the student, the teacher, the parent, the administrator, and the architect are all vital ingredients in the process of educational change.*

Architecture and Education

"Better architecture contributes to better schooling"[21]

The Finnish education system has long been considered one of the best in the world. At the very cornerstone of this education system is classroom design: Finland's schools implement innovative layouts, which are far removed from traditional classroom set up. Reimagining classroom design has allowed Finnish schools to radically reform how students are educated – helping provide individual support and effective collaboration.

The architecture of a school classroom exerts a powerful influence over the utilisation decisions, the behaviours and the interactions that will occur in the space. Professor C Kenneth Tanner of the University of Georgia's School Design and Planning Laboratory (SD&PL) has studied the topic of the influence of architecture on education extensively. His study in the year 2000 covered 14 schools with over 8,000 students and his detailed examination across 39 physical characteristics of the school environment concluded that there was a statistically significant correlation between 7 physical factors and student outcomes - measured as scores on the Iowa Test of Basic Skills (ITBS)[22].

A later study[23] in 2009 compared student achievement with three school design classifications: movement and circulation, day lighting, and (external) views. Evaluated across 71 schools researchers found significant effects impacting Reading vocabulary, Reading comprehension, Language arts, Mathematics, and Science. The author concluded: "There are two immediate values to these studies: educational leaders may use the findings to assess their existing school facilities and determine where improvements will have the greatest impact, or planners may use the findings to guide architects in the design and construction of new educational facilities."

The importance of physical space is not just measured in test outcomes. As noted by David and Weinstein[24], "within the school setting, attachments to objects and places are central to the emotional life of the young child. Environmental experiences in childhood continue to be influential throughout life; therefore, the way a school is designed and built can influence student learning. Built environments have direct and symbolic impacts on children". Similarly, Kunz[25] noted in 1998 that "Planners, teachers, school administrators, architects, and designers must recognize the emerging impressions on students formed by the architecture and physical attributes of spaces within schools".

We believe the ESCotF will not only deliver improved learning, but act as a source of pride for students. For the flagship immersive ESCotF@MGF room, the Entrance area is a friendly space connecting the rest of the school to the advanced inside world. It is inviting, highly visible and evokes a welcoming feeling, with an added element of curiosity.

Investment in schools has long been a global concern. As long ago as 1848, the first US Commissioner of Education, Henry Barnard, wrote in School Architecture that "schools are too small, badly lighted, not properly ventilated, imperfectly warmed, not properly furnished, lacking appropriate apparatus and fixtures, and deficient in outdoor and indoor arrangements" [26].

Since then, there have been international efforts to better align the work of architects and educators as exemplified by the establishment of The Organization for Economic Co-operation and Development (OECD) Program on Educational Building (PEB), which promotes cooperation and the international exchange of ideas, information, research, expertise and experience across all aspects of educational buildings. Similarly, the Association for Learning Environments (formerly the CEFPI - Council of Educational Facility Planners International Foundation) is a non-profit association which aims "to strengthen learning for all through better environments"[27]. These types of initiatives provide useful repositories of international best practices and research conclusions.

School architectural design is, however, still often tied to outdated practices and constrained by public funding limitations. For example, in the US, where a large-scale funds are being invested in school construction, the University of Georgia's School Design and Planning Laboratory (SD&PL), expressed concern about money being spent on the "reproduction of faulty, educationally unsound, and dated architectural designs"[28]. In comparison to many other building types, classrooms are spaces with an unusually demanding set of requirements and are worthy of additional consideration above and beyond the creation of a basic room. As we'll explore in the following sections, constructing an optimal learning space, requires early consideration of many elements.

Size Matters

Other than in a new school build, in most cases the classroom will be a set size and shape, which can tempt education planners to overlook the room itself and move on to the more operational elements of schooling. However, there are several physical factors that can - and should - be assessed and optimised or at least controlled.

For countries experiencing rapid population growth, there has been a temptation to build larger classrooms. A cautionary note though: t research clearly shows high levels of cognitive achievement are rare in large classes and crowded schools[29]. However, any architectural move to physically constrain class sizes can rule out flexible room layouts, space for collaboration and/or individual activity areas, so it's vital not to just look at space in a classroom as capacity for additional desks. Inappropriate use of classroom space can have substantial negative impacts. Too high a density can cause excess stimulation, distraction and stress.

Even in cases where more recent schools have been designed in line with current insights, evolving requirements for improved accessibility and sustainability mean even relatively contemporary buildings should be reviewed for suitability and may require remedial interventions. Encouragingly though, in older schools that may have been constructed without particular emphasis on anything other than the provision of a rudimentary, functional room, there are steps that can be taken to encourage better learning through attention to detail and inputs from specialists in learning space design.

Simple room design touches that can help create a sense of belonging for children were factored into our ESCotF thinking. For example, as highlighted by Meek and Landfried,[30]Crow Island School positioned their door handles at a suitable height for children rather than adults. In line with this intention to create a room at the right scale for children, we've chosen automated sliding doors and positioned all controls within reach, which also fulfils our commitment to accessibility.

Note: Many education researchers have highlighted positive results from the inclusion of outdoor learning and play facilities. Although outdoor learning is outside the scope of this project, we recommend that anyone planning learning spaces, where this is climatically and spatially appropriate, should consider including outdoor elements. For some inspiration, review this video about an innovative Kindergarten in Japan - https://www.youtube.com/watch?v=J5jwEyDaR-0.

The Classroom Environment Impact

The identification of the impact of the built environment factors on learning progress is a major new finding for schools' research, but also suggests that the scale of the impact of building design on human performance and wellbeing in general, can be isolated and that it is non-trivial. Maximising pupils' achievement is an important societal issue.

Barrett et al[31]

Perhaps the most widely read research on classroom environments to date is the seminal work of Professor Peter Barrett. He proposes a three-point framework that reflects: the human "hard-wired" response to the availability of healthy, natural elements of our environments; our desire to be able to interact with spaces to address our individual preferences; and the various levels of stimulation appropriate to users engaged in different activities. His three dimensions, or design principles, have been used to suggest and structure the factors to be considered, namely:

- **Naturalness**: light, sound, temperature, air quality and links to nature;
- **Individualisation**: ownership, flexibility and connection;
- **Stimulation** (appropriate level of): complexity and colour.

While the subcomponents of the naturalness dimension are relatively obvious, his Individualisation principle relates to how well the classroom meets the needs of a particular group of children. Flexibility is a measure of how the room addresses the needs the different age groups that may use a room and any changing pedagogy.

The Stimulation principle relates to how exciting and vibrant the classroom is. Complexity refers to how the different elements in the room combine to create an environment that may be visually coherent and structured, or random and chaotic. Periods of focused attention is crucially important for learning to occur. However, maintaining focused attention in overly stimulating classrooms may be especially difficult for children who are still developing the ability to filter out distractions.

The HEAD Project[32] sought to bridge the gulf between what is a high level of confidence in the literature about some of the different elements and a lack of convincing evidence concerning their combined effects in practice.

The ESCotF project is focused on the educational time of students but acknowledges that, additionally, several external factors (such as domestic circumstances) cumulatively make up the total formative influences on students. The external factors are outside the scope of this book but are also very important.

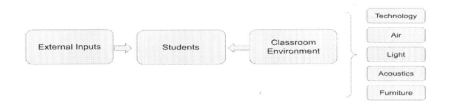

Figure: The broader ecosystem of influences

The HEAD study is far too detailed to cover here but for anyone seeking a deeper understanding, we'd recommend reading it in its entirety. The use of bivariate analysis and multi-level modelling (MLM) to isolate the individual pupil effects from the impacts connected to the school built environment speaks to its statistical robustness, The breakdown of the 3 top level concepts into 10 design parameters which in turn were expanded into eighteen "indicators", underpinned by thirty more detailed, measurable, "factors" shows how comprehensive a study it was, covering some 3766 students in 153 classrooms across 27 schools in the UK. Some study highlights to note were that there was no significant gender correlation and older students showed less benefit from environmental improvements, as did already well-performing students. The most quoted output of the study is the finding that the combined impact of optimal physical characteristics in a classroom could improve academic performance by 16%.

The following chart (based on the work of Professor Barrett) shows how the ideal physical environment is made up from a number of factors:

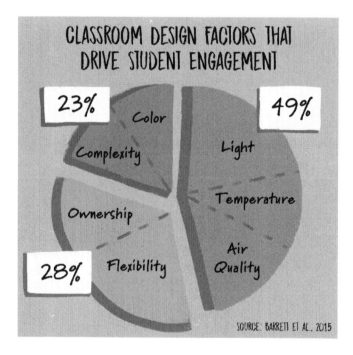

Figure: The key contributing physical classroom factors[33]

We'll examine these features in the remainder of this section.

Beyond the Architecture: Classroom Design & Indoor Environment Quality (IEQ)

Alongside the constructed elements, there are several other physical characteristics that determine the room's suitability as a learning space. As with the architectural elements just discussed, the design & environment are often overlooked in any drive to improve educational outcomes. This may be simply an oversight or an assumption that it is relatively unimportant, or that it might be harder to address than changes to curriculum, delivery method or in-class technology. We see an opportunity to turn the room into an active, explicit participant in the learning process rather than an invisible, perhaps sub-optimal or even negative actor.

Although not widely adopted in many countries where there is significant pressure on education resources, research has shown the importance of an improved environment in learning outcomes. As we conceived the Classroom of the Future, we've carefully considered evidence and expert findings, published in recent years, relating to as many environmental factors as possible, including the air quality, lighting, acoustics and visual stimulation.

Air Quality & Temperature

The SARS-CoV pandemic brought indoor air circulation into mainstream discussions, with organisations such as the Environmental Protection Agency (EPA)[34], Centers for Disease Control and Prevention (CDC) and World Health Organization (WHO)[35] issuing recommendations on the health benefits of improving indoor air quality. Until then, most people didn't realise that indoor air is typically more polluted than outdoor, where the focus on air quality discussions tends to be.

Evidence shows that the air quality in a classroom is an important contributor to academic performance. We'll look first at air quality's academic influence before we look specifically at the health-related benefits.

A 2007 study[36] on the impacts of poor ventilation on cognitive function among school children sets out to quantify the effects of classrooms where optimal ventilation rates are not in operation. Focusing on CO2 levels, the study demonstrates that the attentional processes of school children are significantly slower when the level of CO2 in classrooms is high:

"Using the Cognitive Drug Research computerised assessment battery to measure cognitive function, this study demonstrates that the attentional processes of school children are significantly slower when the level of CO2 in classrooms is high. The effects are best characterised by the Power of Attention factor which represents the intensity of concentration at a particular moment, with faster responses reflecting higher levels of focussed attention. Increased levels of CO2 (from a mean of 690 ppm to a mean of 2909 ppm) led to a decrement in Power of Attention of approximately 5%. Thus, in a classroom where CO2 levels are high, students are likely to be less attentive and to concentrate less well on what the teacher is saying, which over time may possibly lead to detrimental effects on learning and educational attainment. The size of this decrement is of a similar magnitude to that observed over the course of a morning when students skip breakfast."

ESCotF and Indoor Environment Quality (IEQ)

The ESCotF approach to IEQ has two main components - measurement and management.

There's an old management consultancy adage that says, "You can't manage what you can't measure, so measure what matters". The ESCotF will constantly monitor the air quality as shown below. For air management, we specify Child-safe fans including HEPA filtration.

• IAQI	80
• Temperature	17.92 °C
• Humidity	66.20 %
• Abs. humidity	8 g/m³
• TVOC	0.090 ppm
• CO_2	408 ppm
• PM_1	2.2 µg/m³
• $PM_{2.5}$	2.3 µg/m³
• PM_{10}	2.3 µg/m³
• PM_4	2.3 µg/m³
• Noise	63 db
• CH_2O	0.000 ppm
• Light	360 lux
• Pressure	992.65 mbar

Figure: The air parameters tracked in the ESCotF using Atmocube Sensors

Airborne Pollutants

Once again considering the primary users of the room, we note that children are more susceptible than adults to pollutants and other environmental contaminants. Most importantly, they take in roughly twice as much air by volume compared to their body mass as adults, meaning that they also take in twice the pollutants through respiration[37].

It's vital to continuously measure the air quality as what might be satisfactory at the start of a class may have deteriorated significantly by the end. The ESCotF goes beyond the basic measurement and

31

management of CO2, temperature and ventilation rates. Our sensors additionally track the following air characteristics:

- VOCs
- Humidity
- Particulate Matter (PM1, 2.5 and 10)
- Formaldehyde (CH_2O)

The evidence for the importance of these additional parameters includes studies such as the 2015 Harvard research[38] comparing traditional and 'green' workplace designs. We believe these findings are easily applicable to learning spaces, especially as children tend to spend longer in a classroom per day than office workers spend in a similar confined space.

This double-blinded study looked at the impact of volatile organic compounds (VOCs) - chemical pollutants often present in, and released by, paints, cleaning agents, building materials, furnishing, printers, adhesives, markers and many more common materials. VOCs include a variety of chemicals, some of which may have short- and long-term adverse health effects, with concentrations of many VOCs consistently higher indoors (up to ten times higher) than outdoors. The study concluded that the presence of higher levels of VOCs was associated with lower cognitive scores - on average, cognitive scores were 61% to 101% higher in low VOC environments than conventional building settings.

"We found that when participants spent a full day in a Green building, there was a significant increase in their cognitive function scores compared with when they spent a day in an environment that had been designed to simulate a conventional building by elevating VOC concentrations. The study was designed to represent conditions typically observed in many buildings; we did not include extreme exposures or choose uncommon VOC sources."

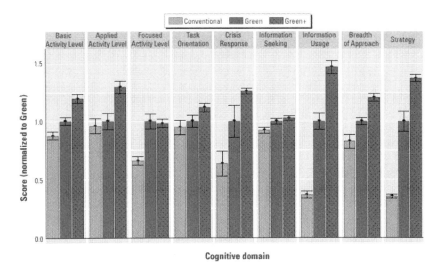

Figure 1. Average cognitive function scores and standard error bars by domain for the Conventional, Green, and two Green+ conditions, normalized to the Green condition by dividing all scores by the average score during the Green condition.

Figure: Comparing cognitive performance in Conventional, Green and Extra-Green environments, showing higher performance in green buildings

Mitigating the risk from VOCs requires choosing materials in the room that have lower VOC emissions, as well as monitoring for the presence of VOCs and increasing ventilation when necessary to reduce VOC levels. ESCotF procurement decisions require suppliers to attest to VOC levels, as well as use of sustainable materials, as we'll discuss in a later section.

It's not just the quality and composition of the air in classrooms that is important. Research has also shown that optimising the temperature can improve educational attainment.

Two field experiments[39] carried out by researchers in 2004/2005 demonstrated improved performance in numerical and language-based tasks by pupils when the classroom temperature was reduced from 25°C to 20°C (77°F to 68°F). When the outdoor air supply rate was increased from 5.2 to 9.6 L/s (11.0 to 20.3 cf/m) per person, student performance of four numerical exercises improved significantly, further confirming the importance of ventilation as discussed above.

Recent focus on energy efficiencies has sometimes led to energy-reduction efforts that prioritise lower use of HVAC. However, at ESCotF, we recommend maintaining HVAC activity at levels that optimise temperature and air quality over reducing energy usage that might compromise educational outcomes. Instead, we monitor the energy requirements to achieve and maintain the desired IAQ levels and ensure that these energy levels are met sustainably.

Health Benefits

Although we're focused on the direct measurable educational impacts of improved air quality, there are obvious benefits in terms of improved attendance if there is a reduction of sick building syndrome due to improved management of air quality.

The SARS-CoV pandemic saw multiple specific studies on transmission in school settings, as well as a focus on remedial measures such as "Ventilation regimes of school classrooms against airborne transmission of infectious respiratory droplets: A review"[40] and "Ventilation procedures to minimise the airborne transmission of viruses at schools"[41].

The CDC's specific guidance for improving ventilation in schools[42] included:

- Bring in as much outdoor air as safely possible.
- Use child-safe fans to increase the effectiveness of open windows.
- Ensure Heating, Ventilation, and Air Conditioning (HVAC) settings are maximizing ventilation to provide acceptable indoor air quality, as defined by ASHRAE Standard 62.1[43]
- Install air filtration systems

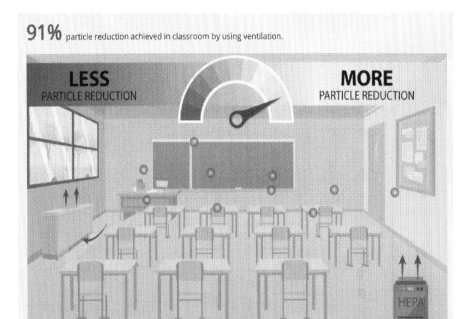

Figure: An illustration from the CDC interactive classroom ventilation tool[44]

The ESCotF design includes all of these measures to maximise air quality and has additional provisions for times of heightened concern regarding air quality, such as periods of elevated respiratory disease circulation. This includes:

- Disabling 'smart' demand-controlled ventilation (DCV) controls that reduce air supply based on occupancy or temperature, instead providing continuous air filtration and distribution.
- The HVAC system at maximum outside airflow for 2 hours before and after the building is occupied to refresh air before arrival and remove remaining particles at the end of the day.
- Installation of pathogen specific detection
- Consider using ultraviolet germicidal irradiation (UVGI) in schools and non-home-based childcare programs as a supplemental treatment to inactivate the virus that causes

COVID-19, especially if options for increasing ventilation and filtration are limited.

EStars is monitoring the evolution of additional technologies such as Far UV (or Far UVG) radiation. As is typical of newer technologies, the evidence for safety is less documented than for more established ones.

Lighting

"lighting is the cheapest and most influential tool that we can use to tap into the subconscious of a person"

Iván Cotado, interior designer[45]

As well as its obvious role in helping us see, light affects us in many other complex ways. It is one of the most important elements in interior design, not only illuminating the space so that we can work but contributing to the ambiance and impacting our biology - helping our bodies produce Vitamin D, as well as impacting our circadian rhythms (these rhythms stimulate hormone production, sleep-wake cycle and core body temperature cycles). Without appropriate lighting, we may additionally suffer eye strain, fatigue, sleep deprivation and headaches.

Many rooms will have an interplay between natural light (typically via windows and/or skylights) and artificial light sources. As a species, we've relied on fire as a light source for millennia before the invention of the lamps in the late 18th century. The era of the more modern incandescent bulb has been largely ended by fluorescent tubes and more recently LEDs, which allow for great control over lighting in a long-lasting, compact, flexible and extremely efficient manner.

Lighting is a major contributor to the atmosphere of a space and should form an integral part of the overall interior design process, factored into the room design from the outset and carefully configured to enable a safe and healthy use of the space. According to Veitch and McColl's 2001 paper, *"Full-spectrum fluorescent lighting: a review of its effects on physiology and health"*, lighting's cognitive and mood-related effects on people have noteworthy implications: (a) better performance on cognitive related tasks in the workplace or academic environment and (b) overall improved quality of life and well-being[46].

Lighting and well-being

As an added impetus to invest in good lighting design, studies have noted the positive impact of good lighting in classrooms both on academic performance and additionally on student well-being. Natural light positively contributes to a higher academic performance in reading as well as in science. It also supports attention, the stability of the circadian cycle and overall health, mental health and comfort, which in turn, leads to better academic performance[47].

Lights of different wavelengths also affect blood pressure, pulse, respiration rates, brain activity, and biorhythms. Quoted in a landmark paper on the impacts of lighting on learning by Mott et al, Tanner reiterated, "Light is the most important environmental input, after food and water, in controlling bodily functions" (as cited in Wurtman, 1975)[48]. A lack of sufficient light and/or prolonged exposure to poor quality artificial lighting can affect people's eyesight. This effect is even more pronounced in children during their developmental years. Mott's study was very wide-ranging as shown in the framework diagram below:

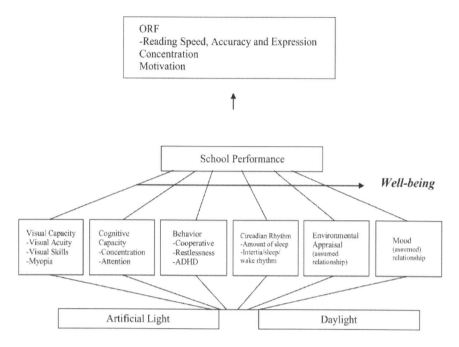

Figure: Mott study framework

Shining a Light on Education

So, alongside air quality discussed above, lighting is clearly another vital element in the classroom environment. Lighting has a big influence on how we learn, so effective lighting design is crucial in education spaces. Thanks to substantial amounts of research, and the emergence of new lighting technologies there is now a much deeper understanding of the relationship between lighting, educational attainment and well-being, as well as much improved options to improve and optimise the lighting levels in our classrooms.

Lighting is, of course, essential to provide safe navigation of space but carefully designed lighting can alter the overall ambience of a space and directly impact the productivity of people - our ability to concentrate correlates with the lighting conditions. Carefully planned classroom lighting increases both the students' attention and well-being. Lighting needs to be functionally bright when required, and flexible, despite varying space utilisations. Lighting affects how the size of a room is perceived and we use it to carefully create ambiance, through a mixture of ambient lighting and task lighting, alongside EStars' unique active lighting, which we use in place of the more traditional accent lighting that interior designers rely on for ambiance manipulation.

Brighter Students

The importance of good lighting in classroom spaces derives from the fact that light doesn't only affect what we can and can't see clearly, but also has an impact on several different physical and emotional attributes. Poor lighting in a classroom can reduce students' capacity to read, reduce concentration levels and lead to both short and long-term visual impairments. Unsuitable lighting in classrooms can also lead to hyperactivity and other behavioural challenges.

Pilot studies, such as those carried out by Professor Michael Schulte-Markwort et al[49], have shown that correct lighting in the classroom, in terms of intensity, colour temperature, and dynamism, helps to increase reading speed by 35%, while, at the same time, reducing comprehension errors by 45%. In the same way, it was also shown that warm lighting reduced hyperactivity in the classroom by up to 76%.

A study[50] of schools in the UK revealed that many older schools still have fluorescent lighting and have not yet upgraded to more modern LEDs. These fluorescent lights can have an imperceptible 100 Hz flicker inside classrooms that can cause "discomfort and impair task performance". The study also found mean illuminance was in excess of recommended levels in 88% of classrooms. Lighting could not be adequately controlled due to classroom design and infrastructure. Ceiling-mounted data-projectors directed at whiteboards resulted in specular reflection from the whiteboard, visible as a glare spot with luminance high enough to cause discomfort and disability glare. Other reports on the impact of lighting in the classroom found links between lighting and attainment, changes in student behaviour and relaxation levels.

"Studies show that overhead cool-white fluorescent lighting ricochets off the surface of a school assignment into the eyes. This reflection causes a type of unintended glare called veiling reflection. This interferes with students' ability to read words on paper and the chalkboard, which in turn harms academic performance. In fact, those classrooms in which natural lighting was used had students performing at about 25% higher rates than their peers."[51]

Natural Light

Note: Although the ESCotF@MGF does not feature any daylight due to its temporary and immersive nature, that should not be taken as an endorsement of classrooms at large not featuring daylight. Daylight plays an important role in the design of classrooms and we strongly recommend all students spend the majority of their day in rooms with natural light which provides physical and physiological benefits.

A 1999 study by Lisa Heschong[52] discovered that students receiving high levels of natural light were achieving test scores significantly higher than students receiving minimal natural light.

"Controlling for all other influences, we found that students with the most daylighting in their classrooms progressed 20% faster on math tests and 26% on reading tests in one year than those with the least. Similarly, students in classrooms with the largest window areas were found to progress 15% faster in math and 23% faster in reading than those with the least. And students that had a well-designed skylight in their room, one that diffused the daylight throughout the room and which allowed teachers to control the amount of daylight entering the room, also improved 19-20% faster than those students without a skylight."

Looking at the influence of daylight on student well-being, a study[53] publishing in 1992 examined the effects of light on the production of stress hormones, classroom performance, body growth, and sick leave, of school children over a period of a school year and concluded that windowless classrooms should be avoided for permanent use.

Changing natural lighting sources after a room has been built is difficult, so it's important to consider building orientation and sun path geometry when classrooms are being planned. This is also influential in managing building temperatures, and in many locations, the potential for solar panels. Thankfully, modern design software, including VR, makes visualising these factors much simpler for (school) architects.

Within a classroom, controls for natural light sources are usually present for use by teachers and students, in the form of blinds, curtains or shutters. However, these are usually deployed on an arbitrary subjective basis. ESCotF includes light meters so that accurate data is used, rather than perceptions or individual preferences. The presence of potentially positive lighting features can be undermined by local decisions or manual interventions - for example, if adequate windows that could allow natural light into a classroom are covered by blinds. Thanks to the presence of sensors and automation, the ESCotF platform is designed to monitor the room in real time and alert any negative variations in the environment. The environmental parameters are recorded continuously to facilitate analysis and, potentially, research.

Artificial Light

Of course, it will frequently be impractical to offer classes with uniquely natural light due to architecture, seasonal variations or other physical factors. There may also be days where there is simply insufficient natural light to provide adequate illumination in specific zones of a classroom. Thankfully, modern lighting technologies offer greater control over light but also much higher quality light than previously available.

Artificial lights allow for greater control of light levels but also the colour temperature of the light. The intensity of light is measured in units called 'lux' while the colour temperature is measured in Kelvin, and ranges from cool (blue/white) to warm (orange/red) light. The combination of intensity and colour determines the impact lighting will have on the occupants of the room.

The Mott study[54] assessed the relationship of lighting quality and colour temperature to the body and mind by testing four distinct light settings in conjunction with Philips SchoolVision lighting platform. The four settings were:

- Normal
- Focus
- Energy
- Calm

Lighting in educational spaces should have lighting that can vary the colour temperature from warm temperatures to promote calmness/relaxation (>2700K) such as when children return from a breaktime, and cooler, more intense lighting (4000K to 5000K) to promote alertness and concentration.

Each of the 4 lighting modes above is designed to correspond with various classroom activities, with the appropriate setting selected by the teacher. Each mode consists of a different intensity and colour temperature. The normal setting can be used "for regular classroom activities," whereas the focus setting can be employed "when children have to concentrate, such as for tests." Energy is a setting designed for use during times of day when students experience a reduction in energy, usually "in the morning and after lunch." Finally, the calm setting is designed for group activities requiring cooperation or supporting the students to settle down when students are "overactive." Consequently, the current study sought to identify effects for SchoolVision focus light setting as it relates to concentration, motivation, and Oral Reading Frequency (ORF).

The study showed students, with the lighting of 6500K and 1000lx showed increased student ORF scores compared to students exposed to lighting at 3000K and 500lx, while results exploring user behaviour and mood test parameters indicate that blue-enriched light increases student concentration and cognitive performance (processing, speed, concentration, and memory).

Full Spectrum Light

Modern indoor lighting solutions mimic daylight by offering full-spectrum light (a spectral distribution similar to that of sunlight), which supports healthy circadian rhythms, unlike standard fluorescent and tungsten bulbs. This can improve academic outcomes by improving students' sleep - well-rested students will obviously be in a better position to learn than sleep-deprived ones. Disrupted sleep patterns interfere with a student's ability to focus in class the next day and diminishes the natural storage and integration of the day's learning that happens during high quality sleep.

Lighting Controls

Ambient lighting refers to the general illumination of the room. Along with the basic lighting it provides, it can also be used to create a sense of warmth and depth in the space. While many classrooms have ceiling luminaires or fluorescent tubes, more diffuse lighting avoids harsh shadows that can make a room seem angular and less welcoming or relaxing. What's known as Task lighting is very important in a classroom - this is non-decorative lighting to illuminate a particular task or activity. This can be challenging from a design perspective given the innate flexibility of the room which can be configured in a number of ways/orientations - ESCotF includes pre-programmed, optimised lighting that has been calibrated for specific uses in the room.

Lighting should not be a one-size-fits-all approach. Classrooms should not have binary on/off lighting options, and even dimming does not sufficient flexibility. The quality of light should be controllable based on the activity, time of day and mood of the children. So while blue-enriched bulbs can improve students' cognitive performance, it is desirable to reduce blue-light exposure later in the day to avoid upsetting natural circadian rhythms. In cases where the classroom is used for afterschool activities, the ESCotF has equipped computers and other devices with screens with an app to modulate the emission of blue-light in the evening.

And, as mentioned above, school rooms with windows may have a large variety of window coverings, from shutters to curtains or blinds. Accordingly, the ESCotF systems have been designed to accommodate a variety of window coverings and includes light sensors to facilitate automated responses to varying light levels. The ESCotF lighting design allows for the careful control of lighting temperature (not to be confused with our air temperature controls!), from 2000K to 6000K, as well as blue-enriched LED lights.

Visual Comfort

Given the length of time that children spend in classrooms, it is especially important to ensure the space prioritises visual comfort, both for their eyes and nervous system, during their formative years. Along with the ability to regulate the light intensity and colour, a classroom should also be assessed to minimise instances of glare.

In the interests of brevity, we won't go into too much further detail here on the intricacies of good lighting design. However, this is a quite technical area and permanent classroom installations should be done in consultation with expert lighting designers who will advise on factors such as: eyelines, intensity, uniformity, flicker, glare and colour. Glare in particular can interfere significantly with visual accuracy and comfort, resulting in eyestrain, headaches and lower educational attainment, while flicker has been associated with triggering epilepsy.

Glare is the visual sensation caused by excessive brightness, and can be either direct or reflected. Although not always apparent in real-time or uniform across different viewing positions in a classroom, glare causes fatigue and eyestrain. Glare should be assessed using what's known as the Unified Glare Rating (UGR) which classifies the glare caused by lighting along a psychometric scale of discomfort. As with all influences in a classroom, the height of children's eyes, along with their heightened sensitivity to blue light makes glare a particular challenge.

ESCotF Active Lighting: Flexibility & Integrations

A key tenet of the ESCotF is flexibility and that extends to the lighting design. The advanced lighting system offers zone-based control that can shift from dim and indirect lighting to direct lighting required for precise tasks, as well as ambient lighting that exudes freshness and positivity.

Based on the lighting-related research mentioned above, EStars has developed a firmly evidence-based approach to lighting in classrooms, before we also added support for dramatic lighting effects during game play. This has led us to create a flexible, adaptive lighting system that is an integral part of the room's operation and ability to support diverse learning activities, while contributing to the children's health and well-being. But we haven't forgotten the importance of making the room exciting, so we've embraced the tendency for game-related use of RGB lighting patterns.

We have further extended the role of lighting in the classroom to include what we call *active lighting* - with guide lighting and status lighting. Our guide lighting can direct the placement of room elements for different layouts by showing the recommended position of each element using floor lights. Our status lighting feature is integrated with the other technologies in the room - for example, giving visual indications for environmental alerts, completion of 3D-printing tasks or drawing attention to the hydroponics bays if they require interventions.

In Camera

Lighting should be primarily designed to provide sufficient lighting for the task at hand in the room but, increasingly, classrooms also require additional lighting to facilitate the recording/streaming of classes for remote learners. Classrooms are no longer the closed spaces they once were, with webcams now a common piece of equipment. The ESCotF is equipped with multiple PTZ cameras to offer full coverage of the space, though with full privacy-respecting protocols in place. Although more expensive cameras can offer excellent low light performance, cameras typically require different light levels than the human eye, so our lighting design and camera configuration takes broadcast and recording requirements into account too.

Acoustics

After air quality and lighting, the next consideration in creating the most effective learning environment is acoustics - the properties or qualities of a room or building that determine how sound is transmitted in it. Just as with the other physical factors under discussion, acoustics is a complex, multi-layered domain that requires early inclusion in room design, along with careful planning, measurement and management. Similar to the other physical factors, the ESCotF looks to incorporate the latest sound-related research and technology to create the environment most conducive to effective teaching and learning, going above and beyond the minimum recommended standards.

Children are more sensitive listeners than adults. They are less able to filter out background noises and less able to use existing knowledge to infer any missing information lost due to poor sound conditions. This makes it more difficult for teachers or school planners to realise how poor an acoustic environment their learning spaces may be for children, as they don't perceive it in the same way that the younger students experience.

Listen & Learn

It might sound obvious, but if students can't hear their teacher and any audio-visual soundtracks clearly, their ability to learn effectively will be impaired. About 60% of school activities in the classroom utilise spoken communication and sub-optimal acoustics can cause significant speech intelligibility challenges. Like the lack of emphasis on air quality mentioned above, sound quality is a frequently overlooked invisible influence on performance. Currently, in the U.S., classrooms can typically have speech intelligibility ratings of 75% or less[55].

Among the primary acoustical issues that can arise in classrooms are *background noise* and *reverberation time*. These two factors are the main issues to be considered in room design. Too much background noise and/or too much reverberation, combined with any amplification of the teacher, will determine the *signal to noise ratio* - how easy it is for the students to focus on the important audio. Classrooms are not intended to be silent spaces; there will always be a level of ambient noise and, at times, periods of high-volume noise. How this noise is managed will determine how much of the teaching material (signal) gets through to students.

Sound Matters

From an education point of view, learning-space designers need to consider Background Noise, Reverberation and Amplification but each of these factors is further complicated by the requirement for the room to be multi-purpose, with varying layouts - this is harder than designing acoustic performance for a single layout.

Without going too much into the technicalities of sound, it's useful to detail some of the most important acoustic design concepts for classrooms. Let's look briefly at each element of the overall acoustic design priorities for them.

Background Noise

Background noise refers to any undesired auditory stimuli that do not relate to the primary source of audio (usually the teacher, another student or a media soundtrack). Other extraneous signals can interfere with the educational material that the students need to hear in order to comprehend.

Background noise can originate either within the classroom (e.g. from HVAC systems, equipment or other children talking) or from external sources (e.g. passing traffic/transit, construction or lawncare). Background noise is measured in decibels (dBA) and in an unoccupied classroom, shouldn't exceed 45dBA.

Reverberation Time (RT)

Reverberation is the persistence of a sound after it originates, due to multiple reflections from various surfaces. An example of a space with a high level of reverberation might be a tunnel or corridor, while a concert hall or cinema will have been treated to create a low level of reverberation. The time it takes reflected sound to dissipate and become inaudible is known as the reverberation time. Technically, reverberation time is the measure of how long it takes a sound to decrease by 60dB after the generation of the sound has ceased. Short reverberation times are important for speech intelligibility. RT is dependent on the overall volume and shape of the room and the surface materials that may reflect sound. A target reverberation time for a classroom is usually between 400 and 500 milliseconds. Longer reverberation times have a disproportionately more detrimental impact for students with hearing impairments than those with normal hearing.

Signal to Noise Ratio (SNR)

The signal to noise ratio is the difference between the desired educational signal (usually the teacher's voice or a video soundtrack) and the background noise where each child is sitting, bearing in mind the background noise may be different at different locations in the room. The SNR for a student should be +15dB greater than the background noise to which they are exposed.

At times, the acoustical environment may not directly impede learning, but it can cause students to become fatigued at a much faster rate due to the constant cognitive load of processing what they hear to filter extra noise and extract the important information being transmitted to them.

Impacts of Poor Acoustics

The World Health Organisation[56] (WHO) lists the physical environment in schools as one of the major elements of health promotion. Among the stressful environmental factors, high levels of noise can cause irritation, encourage aggressiveness, reduce physical and mental performance, and cause discomfort and headaches.

As with the earlier discussion of air quality and lighting, our approach to acoustic design is based on the evidence of rigorous academic studies in the field. Some studies indicate that up to half of all classrooms investigated do NOT meet the minimum requirements for good acoustics. This has been accentuated by the failure to adapt to increasingly prevalent new educational layouts, such as less traditional front-of-the-class teaching and more student-centric activities based on cooperation and active knowledge retrieval carried out in groups.

From a background noise point of view, a landmark research study by eminent environmental psychologists Dr. Arline Bronzaft and Dr. Dennis McCarthy[57] showed that the noise from nearby elevated trains passing a classroom led to students reading scores testing at a level one year lower than students in a classroom on the quiet side of the same school. A follow-up study revealed that after noise-abatement measures were put in place by the transit firm, the reading scores were equal in both classrooms.

Background noise has been shown to impact children's test performance significantly in schools, while children sitting in the back row of a classroom may only hear 50% of their teacher's words. Evidence proves that poor acoustic spaces can negatively affect not only children's learning, but also their mental health. Children exposed to high noise levels at school are more prone to psychological stress and disruptive behaviour. Classrooms with high levels of background noise cause children to struggle with selective attention skills, working memory, and idea generation.

Poor acoustics, whether caused by noise or reverberation or both, can have a negative impact on how students understand speech, how they behave and how well they can concentrate. Children are less adept than adults at deciphering unclear utterances and understanding phrases/meaning when words are missed due to noise or the speech being unintelligible, which means it's vital that all words are clearly enunciated and reach the students without distortion, wherever in the room they may be.

The Acoustical Society of America[58] warns how noise can impact children's learning capabilities: *"Young children are more susceptible than adults to the effects of background noise and reverberation on communication with spoken language. Because of this susceptibility, young children also require more favourable classroom signal-to-noise ratios and reverberation times to achieve the same level of speech intelligibility as adults do. Developmental status, linguistics and cognitive proficiency, temporary hearing impairments, and early receptive and expressive language disorders are all factors that affect the greater susceptibility of young children to background noise and reverberation."*

Another study[59] corroborates the importance of addressing acoustic characteristics of a classroom, citing the importance of minimising noise and reverberation in classrooms, based on the systematic developmental changes in speech recognition in noisy and reverberant environments for elementary school-aged children. The overall pattern suggested that younger children require better acoustic conditions to achieve sentence recognition equivalent to their older peers and adults. Finally for this section, researchers[60]who investigated the extent to which classroom acoustics affected the perceived well-being of students found that long reverberation times, which are associated with poor classroom acoustics as they generate higher noise levels and degraded speech intelligibility, bring pupils to a reduced perception of having fun and being happy with themselves.

Sound Design

Thanks to research and inputs from specialists, there is a range of proven approaches to improving acoustics in classrooms during the design phase, before construction. Even where rooms weren't designed in line with best practices, there are post-construction solutions, such as acoustic wall or ceiling panels, that can be retrofitted to improve the characteristics of sound within a learning space.

Among the guidelines from The Acoustical Society of America, to follow when designing schools in order to improve student performance within the classroom, are the following:

- The maximum acceptable ambient noise levels in the classroom is a steady background noise level of 35 decibels
- The maximum acceptable reverberation time is 600 milliseconds

Where reverberation is a problem, acoustic ceiling tiles can be used to soak up excess reverberation effectively in rooms with ceiling heights less than 10 feet tall. Rooms with higher ceilings will likely require both ceiling tiles and wall-mounted acoustic absorption materials.

Paying attention to acoustics and making conscious design choices or retrospective interventions have been shown to improve learning performance. Addressing both reverberation and background noise levels is demonstrably effective. For example, a 2020 study from Peng et al[61] entitled "Comparative study of acoustical indices and speech perception of students in two primary school classrooms with an acoustical treatment", found the installation of sound absorption materials on ceilings in two primary school classrooms resulted in reduced reverberation time and improved speech intelligibility.

The American National Standards Institute (ANSI) has created a set of standards to be used when constructing and renovating any academic space. While these standards don't necessarily address all the possible issues that could exist in a classroom, they provide a great starting point and can help guide the process of treating the room.

Every day, despite the existence of international standards for desirable classroom acoustics, such as ANSI Standard S12.60 on Classroom Acoustics[62],, thousands of students around the world still attend classrooms that may prevent them from hearing up to a quarter of the words emanating from their teacher. Due to their influence on speech intelligibility, ANSI Standard S12.60 recommends maximum permissible levels for both reverberation time and background noise: under the standard, the maximum reverberation time in an unoccupied, furnished classroom with a volume under 10,000 cubic feet is 0.6 seconds, and 0.7 seconds for a classroom between 10,000 and 20,000 cubic feet. The maximum level of background noise allowed in the same classroom is 35 decibels (dBA), which aligns with The Acoustical Society of America guidelines mentioned above.

Learning Space	Greatest sound level of exterior-sound background noise (dB)	Greatest sound level of interior-sound background noise (dB)	Maximum permitted reverberation times for sound pressure levels from 500 to 2000 Hz (s)
Core learning space with enclosed volume $\leq 10,000\, ft^3$	35	35	0.6
Core learning space with enclosed volume $> 10,000\, ft^3$ and $\leq 20,000\, ft^3$	35	35	0.7
Core learning space with enclosed volume $> 20,000\, ft^3$ and all ancillary learning spaces	40	40	No Requirement

Table 2 Limits on A-weighted Sound Levels of Background Noise and Reverberation Times in Unoccupied Furnished Learning Spaces

Figure: ANSI

Teacher Benefits

While the primary focus on improved classroom design typically revolves around improving learning outcomes, it's important to remember that classrooms are places of work as well as places of learning. For teachers, it's vital to create a healthy workplace that provides conditions for them to function at their best. While we'll focus here on the impacts on student performance, it's also worth noting, as one example, the benefits to teachers of improved acoustics that can reduce vocal strain and fatigue.

There is less research looking at classroom acoustics from a teacher's perspective than from students', but there are some compelling papers showing the various effects of high levels of background noise upon teachers[63]. It is well correlated with teacher fatigue, increased tension and discomfort, an interference with teaching and speech recognition and a significantly higher incidence of vocal problems than is found in the general population.

According to a report from prolific acoustic specialist David Lubman[64], "teachers are less likely to talk with students or will talk with them for shorter periods when noise levels are high", while other researchers warned that high noise levels can bring dysphonia or other vocal pathologies for teachers[65].

ESCotF Sound

The ESCotF is designed to implement best practice acoustic performance on all measures of background noise, reverberation time and signal-noise ratio, with the added focus of achieving this in all room configurations.

ESCotF has an advanced, multi-zone speaker system to deliver carefully controlled sound levels to specific areas of the room. Sound capture via microphones at student stations provides comprehensive microphone coverage. As an additional participation tool for teachers, we're providing novelty throwable microphones that can be used to boost engagement and bring a playful vibe to certain lessons.

The ESCotF also supports behaviour-based sound levels - our measuring of room noise levels, enables teachers to offer students rewards for keeping under a certain threshold, which can help normalise sound awareness for students. Integrated with the active lighting system discussed above, the ESCotF can provide visual signals if noise reaches certain thresholds.

For a more detailed review of the impact of noise in classrooms that looks at 40 years of research, refer to Noise in open plan classrooms in primary schools: A review[66]. For anyone interested in more detail on acoustics in classrooms, the UK Institute of Acoustics offers an exceptionally comprehensive 111-page guide for download[67].

Layout, Furniture, Fittings & Equipment (FF&E)

Now that we've examined the importance of the physical space and the management of air (quality & thermals), lighting and sound, the final part of our physical room discussion relates to what we put in the room and how the contents of the room are to be arranged. The layout and furnishings of a classroom influence how comfortable students feel, how much they engage with teachers and how easily they can engage with one another, both socially and academically.

Classrooms, of course, require seating, work surfaces and learning aids. These items and their interaction with the room and the occupants of the room play a big role in the effectiveness of the room as a learning space. Or, more correctly, we should probably refer to the classroom as a number of learning spaces - a classroom can consist of lots of connected micro-spaces that require different interventions to optimise.

In this section, we'll discuss only furnishings and decorations - teaching equipment will be discussed in more detail in Part 3.

The Importance of Seating

There has been debate over the years about the impact of seating on learning outcomes. Some scholars believe that good students select optimal seats, while others hold the view that the seating choice can help make better students[68]. But, like many other variables in measuring academic achievement, it can be difficult to isolate one specific factor.

A detailed study[69] from 2011 examined the impact of seating locations on a) student learning motivation, b) student-student and teacher-student relationships, c) the nature of different tasks and activities performed, and d) student classroom participation. The paper noted that some of the factors affecting learning experiences and seating selection include student motivation levels, personality traits, the ease of communication, availability of seats, and proximity to learning resources, such as the teacher. Although these factors influence the learning experience, one's ability to recognize such factors will also affect learning success. Teachers may be aware of such conditions, but students are not always cognisant of them.

In a traditional row-based classroom layout, the learning experience received by students sitting near the front of the class is different from that received by students sitting towards the back of the room. The move towards more non-linear layouts is promises to equalise the learning experience more across the space. A 2005 study[70] required students to change seats midway through a course and concluded that the likelihood of achieving an A grade decreased as the distance from the front of the class increased.

Flexibility For The Win

"There is no ideal classroom layout for all activities"

Professor Robert Sommer[71]

As was the case with all of the influences we discussed above, the way a classroom is laid out can also have an impact on how well students learn.

The seminal study by Professor Peter Barrett which we referenced at the start of this section found that classroom flexibility was about as important as factors such as air, light or temperature in impacting student performance. However, the study noted that flexible classrooms are successful because they go hand in hand with a change in pedagogy - the topic of Part 2.

Creating an effective classroom layout is not simply a matter of rearranging tables and chairs - it requires intentional choices regarding the furniture and its position, or more likely positions. Although rows of desks has been the dominant traditional classroom layout, recent years have seen a move towards more creative layouts, as well as different layouts being used at different times. Another interesting concept that has become more prominent is that of 'ownership' - allowing students and teachers agency over the classroom layout so that they feel more involved and in control of the environment, rather than it being a rigid, imposed singular layout.

The adoption of newer pedagogies such as inquiry-based learning (which we'll discuss in Part 2) focuses less on learning facts and more on experiential learning, involving hands-on tasks, collaboration and communication. This new approach to teaching requires supporting changes to educational spaces and how they are configured. Fixed furniture is no longer an option. Learning spaces must be reimagined spatially, being able to support a variety of layouts that can be reconfigured quickly and easily by teachers, with the participation of students.

An interesting element of classroom design and contents is the concept of ownership. Ownership refers to designing a classroom such that students and teachers feel that they own the space around them. This can be accomplished by using furniture that can be reconfigured, even if only to a limited degree, thereby allowing students to rearrange their work environment. It can also be helpful if teachers prefer to rearrange the classroom when switching between lecture style sessions and group work. Researchers believe that involving students in choosing the layout of the room makes them co-owners of the classroom and can also help make the students co-owners of the learning that takes place in the room.

One of the main motivations for deploying novel layouts will be to encourage student participation. Research shows that more students ask questions if arranged in a semi-circular layout looking at the teacher, compared to traditional row layouts[72]. A further benefit of flexible layouts is the ability to create open spaces that enable both children and teachers to walk around. This freedom of movement encourages more collaboration and knowledge sharing, as it creates various additional interaction opportunities.

Devices

In a world of increasing use of digital devices by students in the classroom, the FF&E approach must adapt to this reality. Although classrooms designed even a decade ago perhaps didn't foresee such widespread use of laptops, tablets and other devices in the classroom, it's now vital that classrooms provide accommodations for these devices - charging facilities, storage facilities and the ability to incorporate the devices into lessons. The ESCotF provides not only power for charging throughout the room, but also offers multiple methods for students to share the video output of their device on screens throughout the room.

Although we're focused primarily on pragmatic initiatives to improve learning outcomes, the ESCotF concept is also tasked with considering the future evolution of learning experiences. As we will mention throughout our work, we're closely monitoring developments in AI technologies and in related hardware. Though practical devices are not yet shipping, we know that there will be a range of new AI-infused form factors that purport to be the next generation of post-smartphone devices. It remains uncertain if, how and when these devices may arrive in the classroom, but we are certain that AI-powered personal learning assistants will play a major role in the future of education.

Among the devices that may have to be accommodated in future classrooms, we expect to see students consulting wearable devices and/or desk-based avatars or holograms.

Decorations

Note: The ESCotF@MGF features walls that are entirely LED, so they can be adjusted as desired to change the amount and nature of content. Each of the scenarios (outside full immersion modes) are designed to take account of evidence-based best practices and avoid visual overload or over-stimulation. We've simulated virtual layouts on the LED walls that mimic classrooms to demonstrate implementations for classrooms without displays or projected walls. However, we believe that the potential for large displays to create temporary environments with appropriate visuals will be a powerful primer for learning in future classroom environments.

The wall area of a classroom represents a large surface area and how it is used constitutes an important part of the overall environment of the room. Careful consideration should be given to the use of this precious real estate - among the options available for the walls include:

- Pictures/Posters
- Noticeboards
- Acoustic Absorption Panels
- Smartboards
- Shelving/Storage
- Plain painted surface

Achieving the optimal balance between positive use of this space and creating distracting clutter will be influenced by individual local requirements and preferences of teachers and students, but here we present some of the leading research relating to classroom decor and its role in the educational environment.

The use of wall-space is often left entirely to the classroom occupants (usually led by the teacher) to determine which, although empowering and personal, can lead to the unintentional creation of environments that can undermine the good work that has been put into the other physical characteristics of the room discussed above.

Distractions

Research into the effects of classroom decorations has concluded that heavily decorated classrooms can bombard students with too much visual information, interfering with their memory and ability to focus. A report from psychologists Pedro Rodrigues and Josefa Pandeirada[73], found that overly "sensory-rich [rooms] could hamper children's learning gains rather than help. This study looked specifically at environmental and peripheral distractions, with an aim to identify and support recommendations on how the environment should be organised to foster better daily activities.

The study, carried out in Portugal, was designed to investigate whether a high-load versus low-load visual surrounding environment influences children's cognitive performance, as evaluated by four different cognitive tasks (visuospatial attention and memory tasks). The results suggested that the high-load visual environment adversely affected children's cognitive performance given that children performed better in the low-load visual environment.

The study authors referenced a growing body of work in the space that reflects a recent uplift of interest in the influence of classroom surroundings: Fisher, Godwin, & Seltman, 2014); for example, children's learning environments typically display many colorful materials. Although these stimulating environments are designed to provide sensory enrichment during early phases of development and to motivate *pupils to engage in learning activities (Barrett, Davies, Zhang, & Barrett, 2015), little is known about their real effect in cognitive processes that underlie other activities. Some authors have considered that such environments are "excessively stimulating and disrupting" (Stern-Ellran, Zilcha-Mano, Sebba, & Levit Binnun, 2016, p. 1) and can become a source of distraction (Godwin et al., 2016). Indeed, at a given moment, whereas some of the available stimuli might be relevant to the task at hand (targets), others are irrelevant and may work as distractors (Forster & Lavie, 2014). Attending and processing all visuospatial stimuli is impossible due to our limited processing capacity; this is specially true in children whose cognitive processes are still developing (Gaspelin, Margett-Jordan, & Ruthruff, 2015).*

The study also corroborated earlier work such as Fisher et al.[74] which revealed a decrease in learning gains when the lessons occurred in a highly decorated environment compared to a minimally adorned space. Participants were also more distracted and spent more time off-task in the decorated classroom than in the sparse classroom.

Positive Stimuli

It's worth noting the researchers use of the term low-load rather than no-load. While too much surrounding visual stimuli is not recommended, research also advises against overly bare walls. Barrett et al.[75] found that "The displays on the walls should be designed to provide a lively sense to the classroom, but without becoming chaotic in feel. As a rule of thumb, 20 to 50 percent of the available wall space should be kept clear". They continued to recommend the use of student-created materials, concluding that "students not only feel a greater sense of responsibility for their learning but are also more likely to remember the material".

A further standout is the importance of perspective. "Our findings could be related to the fact that children's cognitive capacities are still under development, including executive functions responsible for the filtering of irrelevant information for a given task," explain the study authors. A teacher may have little difficulty ignoring a wall full of decorations, but young students may find themselves unable to look away to focus on a lesson. The adults designing rooms should always consider the primary users of the room will be the children.

Edutopia[76] provided a useful summary of other recent research on classroom decoration:

- Feature inspiring role models. Putting up images—and short stories or quotes—featuring heroes and leaders can help students gain a greater sense of belonging and aspiration, especially when their backgrounds and interests are represented. Strive for inclusion, but avoid token or stereotypical representations—they can be damaging to students' self-esteem (Cheryan et al., 2014).
- Avoid clutter. Keep at least 20 percent of your wall space clear, and leave ample space between displays so they don't look disorganised. Resist the temptation to keep adding decorations—it's better to swap them out than to keep adding more (Barrett et al., 2015).
- Visual aids—like anchor charts, maps, and diagrams—are OK. Posters that reinforce a lesson, rather than distract from it, can boost student learning. But don't forget to take down ones that are no longer helpful (Carney & Levin, 2002; Bui & McDaniel, 2015).
- Avoid displays of student scores or grades. Many teachers use data walls to motivate students, and while they can work for high performers, they can backfire for struggling students, leading to feelings of shame and demoralisation (Marsh et al., 2014).
- Let in natural light. Don't cover up your windows with decorations unless you have a problem with glare or outside distractions. Students in math and reading who are exposed to more natural light in their classrooms outperform peers who get less natural light (Cheryan et al., 2014). If you don't have

windows, making sure the room is well lit can boost achievement (Barrett et al., 2015).

- Balance wall colours. You don't have to stick with four white walls—try having a single feature wall painted a bright colour, with the rest being muted (Barrett et al., 2015).

Picking up on the final recommendation on the list above, colour is an important factor in room design and ambiance. Building on the definitive book "Color in Interior Design"[77] by John Pile, the ESCotF considers the influence of colour on the occupants of the room. Children may respond differently to colours - some may be overstimulated by bright colours -reds, oranges and pinks are warm and stimulating colours, while most blues and greens are considered cool and relaxing. Most greys are thought of as neutral. Deep tones can make a room look smaller. In the fully immersive ESCotF@MGF, we can vary the wall colours at any time, while in non-immersive rooms, we recommend the use of coloured lighting to change the colour (as opposed to the colour temperature of white light discussed earlier).

The Immersive ESCotF@MGF Room

Some of the concepts shown in the ESCotF@MGF room won't apply to every classroom. While the concept room features full LED wall/floor/ceiling immersion, more traditional rooms will of course feature windows with natural light sources. And in a sign of the importance of natural light, the full immersion room features mock windows with daylight adjusted lighting for when full immersion isn't required.

We would, though, envisage schools having a limited number of such rooms where immersion facilities add genuine educational value. In other cases, we see a role for smart projectors, smartboards and other technologies. But many of the concepts can be applied to more traditional classrooms.

Sustainability & the Environment

A vital ingredient in designing the Classroom of the Future is our desire not only to create the most effective learning environment, but also to reflect our concern for the global environment outside the classroom and the challenge of sustainability. The children educated in an ESCotF will grow up in a world facing daunting environmental upheaval and we are committed to ensuring the ESCotF is at the forefront of sustainability thinking. While this book is focused on where, how and what is to be taught, we have sourced all components for the concept room at MGF mindful of the importance of highlighting opportunities to reduce the carbon footprint of the initiative.

However, the elements of the ESCotF are brought to life in individual schools, which may be constrained by existing built elements, we urge all involved to consider the environmental impact of the operation of future learning spaces and seek to minimise all associated emissions.

Among the sustainability initiatives included in the ESCotF vision are:

- Room power use dashboard
- Power-saving mode on all electronics in the room
- Furniture and Fittings sourced with PCR materials where possible
- Recommended deployment of solar and battery power sources
- Kinetic floor tiles (e.g. https://www.pavegen.com/)
- All schools featuring ESCotF elements to promote recycling and environmentally friendly transport policies

Although outside our current scope, we refer interested readers to some of the initiatives below that are taking place at the school level, rather than the classroom level. Later evolutions of the ESCotF project will continue to closely monitor sustainable technologies and seek to include greener technologies as they become available.

- https://www.americanmodular.com/l-a-s-first-net-zero-energy-classrooms-teach-by-example/
- https://seagrant.soest.hawaii.edu/smart-building-and-community-design/sbcd-projects/net-zero-energy-classrooms/
- https://www.teachengineering.org/activities/view/cub_zero_energy
- https://centresofexcellencenb.ca/energy/?learning_activity=design-a-net-zero-energy-classroom

Building the ESCotF

Establishing causative links between aspects of classroom environment and the factors mentioned in this section is difficult, in part because of the practical and ethical difficulties in conducting controlled trials in classrooms.

We want to review the multiple dimensions of the physical classroom and implement as many evidence-based initiatives as possible, which we believe will be made easier through the use of modern materials and appropriate technologies. We have strived to automate and simplify the sometimes esoteric and highly technical individual influencing factors into a holistic platform that's easy to operate and won't distract teachers in their use of the improved facilities at their disposal.

We also acknowledge that, despite the conclusive data from some research, there remains a need for local adaptation, so we have designed our control systems accordingly. We also note that continuing research around the world is refining findings from prior studies, and we believe therefore that continuous review of even widely accepted findings in light of new evidence, improved methodologies and new realities, is important.

The ESCotF records thousands of environmental data points every day, and these will be analysed to identify further areas for improvement. We assess only room-level data and all data collected by the ESCotF is anonymized and cannot be traced to individual students.

While we look at individual contributing factors, ultimately each student will experience and process a variety of multiple inputs differently. Going forward, we expect AI learning technologies to create a truly personalised learning path for each student, and the ESCotF has an Application Programming Interface (API) concept ready to provide an interface between the student, the physical environment and digital learning materials.

The following diagram summarises our thinking on the physical aspects that will evolve from the classrooms of today on the journey to classrooms of the future.

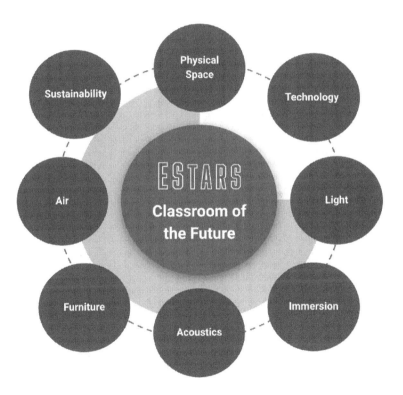

Figure: The EStars Classroom of the Future: Physical Elements

Environmental Designer Anne Taylor refers to the classroom as a three dimensional textbook[78]. This is a lovely metaphor, but hides a complex interplay of influences. In order to make the learning spaces of the future into effective 'textbooks', designers need to holistically address the physical environment as shown above.

This will maximise the contribution of the physical room environment to student educational attainment - the aggregation of even marginal gains might combine to really significant gains in educational performance - and create the best possible chances for the pedagogical methods, which we'll discuss in the next section, to succeed.

Part 2: Teaching Methods

Pedagogy also needs to be combined with expertise in the design of learning environments to get the most out of it.

Changing the layout of your classroom will almost certainly have no impact at all—if you don't change your teaching too.

Edutopia[79]

In Part 2, now, we'll move on to look at the teaching methods that we expect to be employed in the ESCotF. Whereas Part 1 was focused on the 'where' of teaching, Part 2 is about the 'how'. To prepare students effectively for a rapidly changing future, we believe that new methods of teaching will be required. Today's rigid curricula, focused on narrow assessments, will not suffice.

Just as with the physical design we discussed in Part 1, there are numerous studies from eminent educational and cognitive psychologists, identifying improved approaches to teaching, that can be harnessed in the ESCotF. The inherent flexibility designed into the ESCotF physical space and its FFE is an important enabler for implementing the new approaches to teaching, as well as facilitating the inclusion of the new topics/skills we'll cover in Part 3.

While this section isn't intended to be a fully comprehensive review of all the best thinking in modern approaches to teaching, we do include here an outline of the main specifically teaching-related principles that have informed our approach to designing the classroom of the future. Physically, we designed and equipped the room to support as many modern approaches to teaching as possible. In line with the complex and varying needs of each teacher, student group and topic, the room facilitates rather than dictates the teaching method choice(s).

Know Your Audience

It is important to point out that the intended cohort for this project is primarily school children aged 15 to 18. We believe it's critically important to highlight that these are years of rapid change for these young people- and we should reflect that in the evolution of teaching during those years - how we teach, not just the level of material, may need to evolve rather than remaining static from 1st year through to leaving school.

Many experts who study learning believe that several widely held conceptions of learning are wrong, however intuitively correct they may seem. There is little or no evidence to support the popular notion of 'learning styles' and no compelling data to show that people inherently can't learn a particular topic - with the right effort and support, most people can learn most topics. We don't believe in a one size fits all approach to education; rather, we espouse offering varied learning experiences to maximise outcomes for as many people as possible.

Newer cohorts of learners (we'll avoid the marketing term 'Gen Alpha' as it doesn't reflect individuals but is sometimes used to describe those born after 2010) will have a somewhat common social history, and are more likely than previous generations to have widespread technology exposure, although it's dangerous to assume a homogenous level of digital literacy.

The US famously introduced a policy of 'No Child Left Behind' in 2001[80], with the subtitle of the legislation being "An act to close the achievement gap with accountability, flexibility, and choice, so that no child is left behind". With ESCotF, we have a more ambitious target - not only do we not want to leave any child behind, but we also want to create an ethos of MPfE - Maximum Potential for Everyone - a philosophy of inclusion and aspiration to be delivered in the ESCotF.

Figure: Education can't be one size fits all. Source Unknown

Beneficial Buzzwords

For anyone who isn't regularly involved with teaching methodologies, this section may seem dauntingly full of buzzwords. But beneath the apparently complex terms, we're recommending evidence-based approaches that offer genuine and measurable benefits. Just as we don't advocate technology for the sake of it, we aren't recommending change for the sake of it when looking at teaching techniques - the emerging science of cognitive psychology offers guidance on selecting new and augmented teaching methods, though there won't necessarily be a total move away from expository instruction in all cases.

ActiveLearning
CognitivePsychology
Education Pedagogy
UDL
DesirableDifficulties Informal
Metacognition
Andragogy/Heutagogy
Learning Theory Formal
Multiple Intelligence
Challenge Gaming
Based
FlippedClassroom

Figure: A word cloud of Pedagogy-related concepts

Some of the approaches outlined in this section may already have started to move from theory into practice, but none has yet had the widespread adoption and profound influence on education effectiveness that we are seeking. Therefore, we have incorporated features into ESCotF that make it easier to embrace innovative pedagogies, compared to more traditional classroom setups.

Failing to Teach

Proposals to radically change the approach to education are always controversial. Without certainty of success, there is almost always an inertia favouring incumbent methods over unproven new ones. Where we propose the adoption of novel solutions, we do so where there is supporting research or evidence that offers a high probability the change will lead to improved outcomes.

There's an inherent irony in the fact that although we're trying to teach students to be creative and innovative and to learn from failure, the same standards often don't apply to experiments relating to teaching. Yet it can be argued we are failing students if we don't at least *try* to find better ways to improve their learning outcomes, even if some of the methods ultimately fail to deliver the anticipated improvements.

There are parallels here to the ethics of medical testing. In those cases, new treatments are only approved where they are proven to at least match the efficacy of current state of the art (SOTA) treatments. But in medical circles, trials can be stopped early if the results are so clearly positive that it's no longer ethical to continue with placebos. In the education space, we believe responsible experiments should be carried out where there is reasonable hope of success, with ethical oversight, transparent consent and remedial supports in place should they be necessary.

As we discussed in Part 1, there are significant gains to be had from physical and environmental changes that have no risk of adverse outcomes. Similarly, there are low-risk approaches when looking at changes to teaching methods. Significant changes can be made with - we would argue - a robust governance and monitoring framework in place.

At EStars, our approach to innovative teaching strategies starts with a growth mindset. We constantly monitor emerging ideas and the supporting research. We work with our customers to devise practical projects and we scour the globe for technologies that will make a genuine difference. We talk to industry to understand emerging needs. Most importantly, we talk to teachers, students, parents and school administrators to get their inputs and feedback.

The Need for New Pedagogies

Innovative teaching strategies don't always mean introducing the latest and greatest technology into the classroom. Instead, innovative teaching is the process of proactively introducing new [or underutilised] teaching strategies and methods into the classroom. The purpose of introducing these new teaching strategies and methods is to improve academic outcomes and address real problems to promote equitable learning.[81]

As curriculum policies in many countries shift to include new domains, skills and competencies relevant to 2030 and beyond, supporting pedagogical innovations must be identified and deployed. Competences such as collaboration, persistence, creativity, and innovation are not so much taught as intrinsic to different forms of teaching and learning through pedagogy[82].

As we understand more about how the brain learns, as new generations of children with distinct characteristics emerge and as we need to teach new subjects, new skills that are crucial for the disrupted world and workplaces of the future, it stands to reason we should adapt how we teach. The major changes required in our curricula to address new learning objectives will require pedagogical innovation if they are to succeed. As we shift focus from the knowledge transfer/rote learning styles of the past to enabling competencies and creativity, our pedagogic styles must look to foster these so-called 21st century skills if we are to equip our children with the relevant skills and adaptability.

Complex Curricula - An OECD perspective

As pointed out in the 2018 OECD report, Teachers as Designers of Learning Environments: The Importance of Innovative Pedagogies[83], "the common education policy variables of structures, regulation and institutional arrangements, and resourcing are relatively far removed from the classroom where learning gains are achieved. The pressures to revamp what we teach *(the focus of Part 3 of this book)* must be preceded by pedagogical innovations that set schools up for success as expectations rise around educational attainment.

In focusing on the role of teachers as creative professionals, the report calls for a highly deliberate form of teaching that promotes student centeredness and active participation as well as "New ways of measuring outcomes that are broad enough to capture 21st century skills and other non-academic outcomes are an imperative for identifying how innovative pedagogies work, and under which conditions".

The field of Pedagogy has become dramatically more complex as the amount of research in the area has increased, catalysed by the concomitant progress in cognitive psychology and the inexorable rise of new technologies. This more rigorous approach will yield valuable direction as we look to ensure our teaching methods evolve and improve.

The OECD also noted that "curriculum policy strategies in many countries now include explicit recognition of what are often called 21st century skills. Yet acquiring competencies such as collaboration, persistence, creativity, and innovation depends fundamentally on the modelling of the teaching and learning itself i.e., pedagogy. If the 21st century competencies are to be systematically developed, rather than being left to emerge by accident, then pedagogy must be deliberately designed to foster these competences - innovative, rather than established, pedagogies can play an important role in this.

Learner-centred pedagogies, such as inquiry-based learning that we discuss below, are particularly suitable for giving learners a more active role and promoting the development of applicable key skills and behaviours.

Teacher-led demonstrations and the presentation of foundational information remain highly relevant but must now be framed with the ultimate objective of promoting students' performance and their active role and participation in solving tasks using extensible frameworks that they can re-apply in the future.

Assessment of such flexible competences requires a shift from a focus on retention of specific knowledge to demonstrable mastery of capabilities.

Importantly, despite the emphasis on developing competencies, this must not come at the expense of students still receiving content/knowledge and achieving a deep grasp of foundational concepts. Hence the chosen pedagogies must support the simultaneous coverage of content and developing the modern transversal competencies that the future demands.

The Seven Principles of Learning

In 2010, an OECD report[84] listed 7 useful principles of learning to help establish a reference for best practices:

1. Make learning central and encourage engagement and awareness in students of their own learning strategies.
2. Ensure that learning is social and often collaborative.
3. Be highly attuned to motivations and the emotions involved in learning.
4. Be acutely sensitive to individual differences, including in prior knowledge.
5. Be demanding for each learner but without excessive overload.
6. Use assessments consistent with the main goals for learning, with a strong emphasis on formative feedback.
7. Promote horizontal connection across learning activities, across subjects, and across in- and out-of-school learning.

Since then, the accelerating pace of technological change has made it essential to reconsider this list. We believe it is important to specifically call out the role of technology and have added the following additional considerations to our use of the core principles:

8. Embrace appropriate technology to augment learning
9. Recast the curriculum and pedagogical tools to support Vision 2030 and beyond
10. Apply learnings from cognitive psychology that demonstrably improve learning outcomes

Pedagogies in Practice

Although there are many definitions of pedagogy, we see it as part of a holistic, circular process aimed at optimising the learning system. As illustrated below, learning is shaped by the classroom environment, which impacts the pedagogies available. The pedagogies are influenced by the available technologies, the application of cognitive psychology of learning and the desired outcomes (i.e. the future-ready knowledge, skills and competencies). These inputs will determine the educational outcomes that the students attain. The system should be carefully monitored to identify opportunities for improvement that can be fed back into the process.

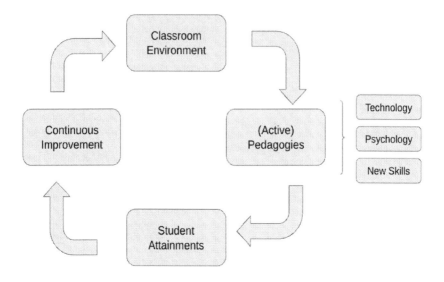

Figure: EStars Pedagogy in Practice

However, we don't want to make the whole process seem overly sterile. As we have said elsewhere in this book, teaching and learning are human pursuits. Effective pedagogy is an inscrutable mix of art, science and craft.

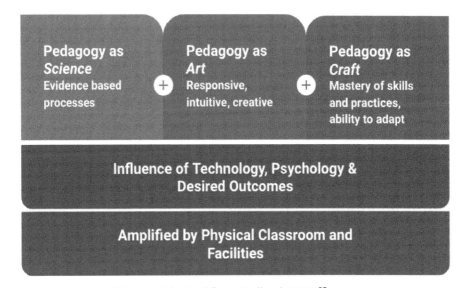

Figure: Adapted from Pollard, 2010[85]

The Key Teaching Trends

A quick literature review will reveal a large and growing body of research into identifying and quantifying new pedagogical approaches. It also highlights investigations into more specific terms such as Andragogy (adult learning) and Heutagogy (self-directed learning). Here, we'll use the term pedagogy to refer more generally to the method/practice of teaching. From these studies, we've extracted the most relevant and rigorously evaluated ones for discussion here but provide references for anyone seeking more detail.

A useful 2019 report from Herodotu et al[86] offers a framework for selecting pedagogies for review consisting of the following five dimensions:

A. relevance to effective educational theories
B. research evidence about the effectiveness of the proposed pedagogies

C. relation to the development of twenty-first century skills (e.g. critical thinking, problem solving, collaborative skills, innovation, digital literacy, and adaptability)
D. innovative aspects of pedagogy
E. level of adoption in educational practice

For example, a 2015 report produced by The Open University in collaboration with SRI International, proposes ten innovations that are already in currency but have not yet had a profound influence on education[87]. Other reports list varying numbers of innovations and changing terminology, but most can be broadly grouped by their particular approach to involving students and moving away from traditional teacher-centric modes.

Although it's not easy to isolate and compare the impact of different teaching methods, a meta-analysis in 2022[88] reviewed 75 studies on teaching methods and identified 4 categories of note when evaluating different teaching methods:

- differences in students (e.g., achievement level, cognitive level, level of previous familiarity with method)
- differences in teachers (e.g., professional experience, subject-specific knowledge, knowledge of the method used)
- differences in context (size or composition of student group, physical classroom context)
- differences in content (school subject and quality of the teaching program)

In this section, we'll look at active learning in general before briefly describing some of the active approaches available including Flipped Classroom, Challenge-Based, Inquiry-Based and Problem-based learning.

Active Pedagogies

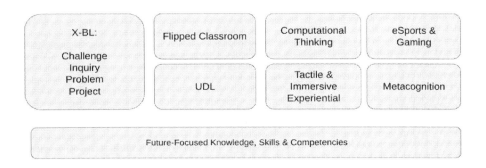

Figure: The EStars Active Pedagogies Framework for the ESCotF

Active Learning

Perhaps the most important pedagogical trend to emerge in recent years is the interest in Active Learning. According to the 2018 OECD report Teaching for the Future: Effective Classroom Practices To Transform Education[89], Active learning is defined as any teaching method that "involves students in doing things and thinking about the things they are doing" (from Bonwell and Eison, 1991[90]).

The age-old concept of a teacher standing at the front of a classroom full of students, lined up in rows, listening to information while watching a (smart)whiteboard, is increasingly a thing of the past. Much more active *learning spaces* will supersede the typical classroom that we know today. This will see students become participants in their own learning.

Active learning differs from more passive traditional listening-based classes by involving the students in the learning process with interactive or experiential contributions. Students are also encouraged to reflect on what they are expected to have learned. The OECD report points to a growing body of empirical evidence indicating that active learning practices are associated with higher academic achievement and notes that students who actively use higher-order thinking skills (such as analysis, synthesis, evaluation, and planning) during the learning process, consistently outperform those who do not actively do so. The latest data from OECD's PISA (Programme for International Student Assessment) shows that cognitive-activation instruction (an active learning technique) is associated with an average increase of 19 points in mathematics scores, across OECD countries, after accounting for other teaching strategies. Other sources show that incorporating active learning strategies into courses significantly enhances student learning experiences[91] and the latest research on learning also demonstrates that students learn more and earn higher grades with active learning[92].

It is also noteworthy that leading higher education institutions (eg Stanford, Cornell and Harvard) deploy active learning principles widely, so students who have been exposed to these techniques at high school level will be able to acclimatise more quickly if they pursue further education[93].

Higher education is bombarded constantly by new applications, new devices, new platforms, and other educational technologies that promise to revolutionise teaching and learning as we know it. Oftentimes, these technologies are purchased, adopted, and/or implemented without any systematic empirical evidence that demonstrates clear benefits for either teaching or learning, or both. Fortunately, Active Learning Classrooms are the one of the few educational technologies for which considerable research-based evidence has been produced, supporting its efficacy for both students and teachers.

But, at the same time, studies on the efficacy of active learning have highlighted the potential for failure or disappointment if the new teaching approaches aren't implemented in a conducive physical setting.

Researchers at North Carolina State University on students in active learning classrooms showed that they outperformed their peers who studied in traditional classrooms, finding positive and significant impacts on an array of outcomes including attitudes, attendance rates, problem-solving skills, and conceptual understanding[94].

Where Active Learning approaches are deployed, it is important to explain the principles to students and parents. Those unfamiliar with active learning can find it disconcerting compared to traditional methods. The shift in emphasis to student involvement in, and ownership of, the learning process can come as a shock. Teachers should make clear to students how the activities relate to stated learning outcomes and what the expectations are for participation (e.g. via polls) and assessments.

Modernising Assessments

Although somewhat beyond the scope of this current volume, it would be remiss not to highlight the importance of reimagining the approach to assessment. As we change where, how, what and why we teach, we must also adjust quantification of success.

As Cynthia Luna Scott points out[95], memorization of facts can no longer be the measure of educational attainment. Future-ready students will require the ability to work in agile teams, harnessing technology effectively, generating new ideas and continuously updating their knowledge, by unlearning and relearning, by mixing formal and informal learning.

Although there is widespread acceptance among educational policy makers that there is a need to ensure educational systems adapt to empower students with the new skills and competencies they will need to thrive in a rapidly changing world, it is challenging to modify the complex, dynamic education system, frequently resource-constrained and focused on incumbent assessment metrics.

Assessment is inextricably linked to instruction and should be used to inspire deeper learning. The OECD report notes that to evaluate deeper understanding, it is essential to assess the extent to which learners' knowledge is integrated, coherent and contextualised. It is not possible to address the issue of transforming twenty-first century instruction without also addressing formative assessments – assessments that enable a teacher to evaluate learning while it is occurring.

Carneiro (2007)[96] notes that people will face meta-learning challenges throughout their lives. They will likely include learning to organise multiple sources of information, learning to learn from experience and deal with the social dimensions of knowledge formation, learning to self-regulate time and effort to learn, learning to forget and to un-learn whenever necessary, and learning to make room for new knowledge.

The ESCotF is ideally suited to active learning through both the flexible physical layout and the extensive range of technology that is present to support and facilitate learning. Taking into account the requirements for most active learning approaches, the ESCotF is designed to help students to engage in their learning by thinking, absorbing, investigating, experiencing and creating, giving students multiple avenues for learning. Active learning does not mean that we should simply abandon teacher-directed instructional learning - the ability to listen is a core component of effective active learning and, as we discussed in the section on Acoustics, ESCotF prioritises quality verbal communication.

Recognising that just because active learning is being used doesn't guarantee improved learning, attempts to employ active learning should also include suitable knowledge checks and achievement milestones. EStars also recommends that active learning pedagogies be combined with proven concepts such as Desirable Difficulties[97].

The ESCotF includes a Nudge mode with the display of helpful hints, deadlines and other useful prompts to remind students of their role in active learning. Teachers can choose which messages to display to students based on the activities taking place. We've also taken this a step further to offer an Incidental Learning mode where we randomly present facts or insights; the walls of the immersive ESCotF are a great learning canvas - people don't even realise they're learning but can engage with the walls.

The Role of Technology in Pedagogy

"Technology's educational role is as an enabler. Pedagogy is at the heart of what makes the magic in classrooms."

Bharat Anand

Vice provost for advances in learning, Harvard[98]

The ESCotF could appear at first sight to be a technology-led project. However, it was conceived from the outset to have a sound pedagogical foundation. We know that technology, parachuted into classrooms without sufficient thought as to the pedagogical implications, is unlikely to lead to the desired improvements in learning outcomes.

We incorporate technology into the ESCotF only after asking ourselves if it can add meaningful new experiences that are clearly aligned with an educational benefit. We appreciate that educators may be hesitant, based on previous experience of unsubstantiated technological initiatives, which is why we have taken so much care to consult policy makers, futurists, teachers, industry partners, parents and students to create an effective learning space that's fit for the future.

We firmly believe that technology, used appropriately, is a vital part of the future of education. Technology will play a complex dual role, both as a learning facilitator and also as a subject of learning itself. Its relationship with curriculum development will be further complicated by the expected emergence of increasingly personalised or adaptive learning solutions that flex for each student.

Technology in education is, of course, a rapidly evolving space and continuous research and adaptation is required. In a study at the University of Dammam[99], the author noted "significant increase in the academic achievements in the students using the technology" and concluded that "Further research is warranted". We agree!

Although related to an older age group than ESCotF, we have analysed with interest the academic research from initiatives such as the Harvard Future of Teaching and Learning Task Force (FTL)[100] both from the point of view of identifying any relevant observations that might trickle down to lower age groups, but also with a view to a greater understanding of how we might better prepare and equip students who will go on to further and higher education.

The Future is Flipped

Flipped classrooms are one of the leading learner-centred active learning models. According to Ağırman, N., & Ercoşkun, M. H.[101],the exact history of the emergence of flipped classrooms is unclear, but one of the biggest foundations for the concept was the 1993 publication "From Sage on the Stage to Guide on the Side" by Alison King, which argued for the use of classroom time for more active learning. But it wasn't until 2007 that the model became more widely adopted, even though it still remains a minority method.

The underlying premise of Flipped Classroom (FC) is that students should undertake assigned learning on the theoretical aspects of a topic in their own time outside the classroom, then come to the classroom prepared to ask questions based on the material and to engage in active discussions or exercises. This is a reversal of the traditional approach where a teacher explains the concepts in class and students complete the exercises as homework. The aim of maximising the precious collaborative but limited time spent in the classroom is a fundamental tenet of the ESCotF, where both students and teachers can use the time most effectively. So, in order to get the most out of the ESCotF, preparatory learning activity also needs to happen outside the classroom.

A teacher's interaction with students in a flipped classroom can be less didactic and significantly more personalised, while students are more actively involved in knowledge construction and processing as they demonstrate, evaluate and refine their comprehension in class.

Among the benefits of the FC can be that students move at their own pace, allowing, them to absorb foundational concepts through readings and/or video materials that can be re-read/paused rather than at the one-size-fits-all pace of an information transmittal-model of direct instruction in a classroom. Teachers can then facilitate higher order discussions or clarifications in face-to-face class time in ways that boost engagement, as students actively and interactively cement and apply that knowledge, resulting in deeper learning.

Another rationale for FC is that it can help offset cognitive overload that can be common in traditional direct instruction classrooms where students are introduced to significant quantities of new information in a short space of time, leaving them little time to process and assimilate it based on their pre-existing knowledge. A 2015 study[102] outlined the relevance of cognitive load theory and concluded that flipped approaches may improve student motivation and help manage cognitive load to improve learning outcomes.

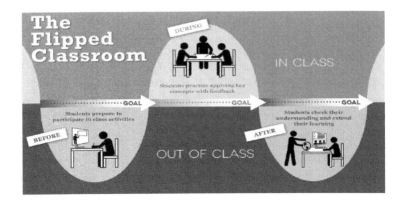

A flipped classroom is one example of more active learning.
Figure: University of Texas[103]

Flipped vs Traditional

An obvious question for anyone considering the move to flipped classroom teaching is how it compares to traditional methods. A 2018 study at the University of Jordan[104] comparing student achievement between the two approaches showed statistically significant increases in student grades in the experimental group using flipped learning. While the study focused on grades, it also anecdotally noted desirable improvements in softer skills. But, although many studies have shown positive results, other studies have shown no discernible difference in grade outcomes between methods, suggesting that there remains significant variance across implementations and that a move to flipped classrooms doesn't offer a guaranteed improvement in all subjects and circumstances.

X-Based Learning

Alongside Flipped Classroom, there are several similar-sounding teaching methods that have emerged as potential approaches to creating more active and engaging lessons aimed at eliciting more future-ready skills. From inquiry-based learning to problem-based learning, project-based learning and challenge-based learning, we've opted to refer to them here collectively as X-based Learning or XBL. Some of these methods can be individual or collaborative in nature, but all are learner-centric. While much has been published about the differences between each method, for the sake of brevity, we'll look here only at key characteristics of each - anyone intending to deploy any of these approaches should conduct some deeper research on their suitability for the intended context.

The ESCotF advantage is that it is designed as a dynamic working space, where students and teachers can use various modern approaches to learning as suits the context.

Challenge Based Learning (CBL)

Challenge-Based Learning is a teaching approach that has gained some traction in recent years. A flexible learning space such as ESCotF is an ideal format for such learning as the room can be (re)configured to facilitate collaborative group work or individually-focused exercises.

"Today's high school curriculum presents students with assignments that lack a real-world context and activities that lead to uninspired projects and end in a letter grade. Many students either learn to do just enough to get by or they lose interest and drop out. In this interconnected world, with ubiquitous access to powerful technology and access to a worldwide community, new models of teaching and learning are possible."

Apple, Challenge Based Learning White Paper[105]

Challenge Based Learning was developed by Apple, working with several leading education experts as part of a larger collaborative project initiated in 2008 called Apple Classrooms of Tomorrow—Today (ACOT2) to identify the essential design principles of the 21st century learning environment, with a focus on high school.

Although some of the original technology aspects are now slightly dated, much of the underlying approach remains valuable, and we believe can be amplified with ESCotF thinking. CBL includes the following attributes:

- Multiple points of entry and varied and multiple possible solutions
- Focus on the development of 21st century skills
- Focus on universal challenges with local solutions
- Requirement that students do something rather than just learn about something
- Documentation of the learning experience from challenge to solution

These attributes were designed so that Challenge Based Learning engages learners, provides them with valuable skills, spans the divide between formal and informal learning, and embraces a student's digital life. CBL aims to provide a framework for acquiring academic knowledge and developing durable skills such as critical thinking, creativity, communication, collaboration, and lifelong learning.

Challenge Based Learning follows a workflow that mirrors the 21st century workplace. Students are given enough space to be creative and self-directed and at the same time are provided with support, boundaries and checkpoints to avoid frustration. The workflow can be structured and modified in a variety of ways. It can be applied broadly across subjects or used as a framework for specific capstone projects, either individually or collaboratively.

The CBL process (illustrated below) starts with a big idea and then moves through stages from an essential question, a challenge, a solution, and evaluation. According to Apple, the big idea is a broad concept that can be explored in multiple ways, is engaging, and has importance to high school students and the larger society. Examples of big ideas are Identity, Sustainability, Creativity, Violence, Peace, and Power.

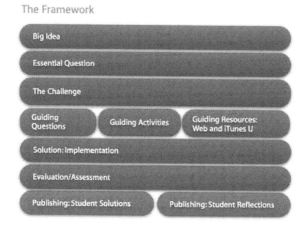

The Challenge Based Learning Framework. Figure: Apple

CBL & Industry

An important aim for ESCotF is to better align the classroom environment and what happens in it with industry needs. Given that a key design goal for CBL was to better align classroom practices with employer needs, it's interesting to note research from Mexico that looked at the importance of involving companies in CBL programmes[106].

The study found that a CBL experience with an industrial partner increased complexity and uncertainty levels and consequently, the development of skills (cross-disciplinary skills, such as teamwork/collaboration, critical thinking, ethics, problem-solving, planning ahead and resilience) was consistently higher compared to learning delivered via traditional methods. In line with these and similar findings, EStars has consulted with industry in the choice of technologies to be deployed in ESCotF to ensure the room can support industry-linked CBL initiatives.

Finally, for educators interested in understanding more of the cognitive science behind an approach such as CBL, a comprehensive 2023 article[107] explores the educational neuroscience behind CBL - studying how the brain learns and processes information and how this knowledge applies to improving teaching practices, learning environments, and educational outcomes. The author describes Fourteen areas in Mind Brain Education (MBE) science that intersect with and support the efficacy of the CBL framework.

Inquiry Based Learning (IBL)

Another popular active learning style is known as Inquiry-based learning, a format that aims to develop critical thinking and problem-solving skills. Rather than lecturing children, the teacher poses questions and scenarios which the students then research individually or in groups and present their findings. This method has the added benefit of developing presentation skills and enabling children to participate in peer-learning.

Studies show that people learn particularly well when they are able to create their own meaning. Through inquiry-based learning, students think about what they've learned, the process, and how to use the same process in future. Engagement is substantially increased and, therefore, so is the learning experience compared to traditional teaching strategies where students are expected to just listen and answer teacher questions and, as a result, are not likely to inquire or ask questions themselves. Inquiry-based methods are suited where the expected learning outcome requires students to develop deeper and transferrable conceptual understanding of topics.

Unlike Challenge-based learning, students are not expected to present a solution, but an original analysis of an event or situation. Unlike traditional instruction where they rely on what they are being told, in IBL they perform activities that generate knowledge, ideally with evidence from multiple sources. Students share their approaches and conclusions with classmates and can face critical questions from each other, in order to strengthen the learnings. IBL can be combined with computational thinking as a framework to guide the students' inquiries.

For optimal results, inquiry-based learning should only be commenced when a student has some foundational prerequisite knowledge but a detailed knowledge is not necessary[108]. Research has also shown that reading comprehension predicts the level of inquiry skills in elementary school children[109].

According to de Jong et al,[110] "another rationale for particular combinations of direct instruction and inquiry is that direct instruction without sustained engagement and practice is insufficient for robust acquisition and maintenance of learning over time (Dean & Kuhn, 2007). These findings align with work on desirable difficulties (Schmidt & Bjork, 1992) and classroom research in which direct instruction led to fewer errors during learning, but ultimately turned out to be less effective on delayed assessments (Vitale, McBride, & Linn, 2016). Thus, direct instruction requires subsequent sustained practice, typically involving some form of student inquiry to produce durable understanding".

Inquiry-based vs Direct Instruction Methods

Frequently pitched in research as a binary choice that tries to pick a 'winner' between traditional direct instruction and newer inquiry (or challenged-based) techniques, there is heated academic debate over their relative merits.

We prefer to see them as complementary, with a valuable role still existing for traditional knowledge transfer. Foundational knowledge and signposts are often still essential to successfully navigate newer pedagogies successfully. Author E.D. Hirsch argues in his book, Why Knowledge Matters: Rescuing Our Children from Failed Educational Theories[111], that the overreliance on skills has produced a knowledge deficit and that it is time to reinstate the value of knowledge in education.

We believe that learning is a continuum, and in each stage of a student's learning, there needs to be a balance between their knowledge and the competencies that they acquire with that knowledge. As we've said, the ESCotF is intended to facilitate different pedagogical approaches, using the physical space and available technologies, to enable the most appropriate and effective teaching methods on an individual teacher and session basis.

In fact, a comprehensive recent study[112] points to the merits of combining active learning and direct instruction techniques as being particularly effective. The authors conclude that a more complete and correct interpretation of the literature demonstrates that inquiry-based instruction produces better overall results for acquiring conceptual knowledge than does direct instruction, but that inquiry-based and direct instruction each have their specific virtues and disadvantages and that the effectiveness of each approach depends on moderating factors such as the learning goal, the domain involved, as well as students' prior knowledge and other student characteristics.

In a meta-analysis comparing inquiry-based instruction and direct instruction on the basis of 164 primary studies, Alfieri, Brooks, Aldrich, and Tenenbaum[113] concluded that unassisted (or unguided) discovery is less effective than explicit instruction, but that assisted inquiry is more effective than explicit instruction involving "explicit teaching of strategies, procedures, concepts, or rules in the form of formal lectures, models, demonstrations, and so forth and/or structured problem solving"

Thus, we hope that the teachers in the ESCotF will take the opportunity to reflect on the learning methods available to them and use their professional judgement to maximise outcomes. Ultimately, the goal of adopting new teaching methods should be to ensure we are equipping students with the skills relevant for the jobs of the future.

PBL

Problem-based learning (PBL) and Project-based learning (PjBL) are other active learning modalities we'd expect to see deployed in the ESCotF. Hailing from the medical education space in the late 1960s,[114] PBL was created to aid students in developing effective reasoning skills, built on constructivism - a learning theory that emphasises the active role of learners in building their own understanding. PjBL traces its origins even further back to the evergreen writings of John Dewey[115].

However, their more modern cousin, challenge-based learning, typically seeks to incorporate development of more 21st-century skills into problem-based learning approaches and emphasises the use of technology to increase its relevance.

In problem-based learning, students are expected to arrive at a known, predetermined solution or conclusion. The problem is usually presented to students before the related content is taught. This is intended to prime students for learning - requiring them to think about the potential solutions, rather than having the solution presented to them. Project-based methods usually expect students to be more creative in presenting a project deliverable that is expected to be original and demonstrates mastery of content, often across multiple disciplines and a longer timeframe than PBL.

According to the evidence[116], the use of PBL is desirable to develop the following skills:

- Working in teams
- Managing projects and holding leadership roles
- Oral and written communication
- Self-awareness and evaluation of group processes

- Working independently
- Critical thinking and analysis
- Explaining concepts
- Self-directed learning
- Applying course content to real-world examples
- Researching and information literacy
- Problem solving across disciplines

Over the years, as summarised by Hopper in 2018, [117] researchers have identified shortcomings in the PBL approach and proposed refinements to improve learning outcomes, such as a more flipped-classroom style approach (referred to as Case-Based Learning in medical circles) that requires students to develop a knowledge base prior to exposure to problems. ESCotF can support PBL approaches with its flexible layouts, simulation technologies and experiential facilities.

Aligned with EStars' belief in the importance of learning to learn, we recommend that active learning approaches be introduced to the classroom carefully - relying on this method too early in the students' academic career may have negative outcomes.

Regardless of the exact X-BL moniker used, expecting students to grapple with and solve an array of relatable projects/challenges/problems, will be a crucial element of future-focused education.

As with the other approaches discussed herein, the most important consideration is the evidence and potential for improved outcomes. According to Kristin De Vivo[118], Executive Director of Lucas Education Research, a series of rigorous studies shows that authentic, student-driven approaches to project-based learning improve student outcomes. Additionally, De Vivo cites that new research found that teachers benefited rather quickly from having strong PBL curricula aligned with high-quality professional development opportunities. In the AP study, for example, the PBL curriculum had robust effects on student performance after just one year of implementation, though the gains were larger when teachers had two years of experience with the curriculum (Saavedra, Rapaport, et al., 2021[119]).

Computational Thinking

Computational thinking encourages students to apply the principles of coding beyond just computer studies. It espouses the development of logical, process-driven approaches to problem solving in a range of domains, enabling children to tackle complex problems in a structured and extensible manner. Students are encouraged to break problems down into smaller units (subroutines), identify precedents that can be reapplied (functions), develop steps that will contribute to a solution (algorithms) and validating/refining their work (testing & debugging). This methodical approach can be applied as a framework for problem solving, and illustrates the value of a toolset mentality so students can confidently engage in novel challenges, within what Vygotsky termed the Zone of Proximal Development[120].

Kinesthetics/Learning by Doing

Kinesthetic or tactile learning where students get to see/try real technologies and 3-D learning aids is a key pillar of the ESCotF experience. Providing students with access to authentic examples of technologies, devices and specialised equipment they will encounter in work and later life is an increasing priority for progressive educators. It is important to narrow the gap between the classroom experience and the real-life experiences students will have in the workplace. Previously only introduced in higher education, it is now possible - and desirable - to insert high tech apparatus into earlier years of the education system. Expanding access to e.g., robotic arms not only enables direct operational training, but also improves conceptual understanding and engagement compared to solely theoretical/descriptive sessions.

Where real world access isn't possible, (e.g., for some chemical or biological laboratories), the sensorial advances in Virtual Reality we'll discuss in Part 3 offer exciting possibilities for educators. In this space, we also include what is sometimes known as embodied learning, that focuses on the role the body plays in learning, as well as the mind. Although outside the scope of the ESCotF project, there are exciting developments to be aware of in harnessing biometric sensors and computer vision in areas such as sport/physical education.

There has also been some interest in the use of wearable and observational technologies such as computer vision and eye trackers to analyse if and how students are learning. This has been met with controversy[121] and ESCotF does not implement any such features.

Gaming

As outlined above, preparing students for the world of 2030 and beyond will require many additional teaching methods. It will be important to harness relevant and engaging methods that both resonate with students and deliver valuable skills.

It's instructive to look at how businesses go about developing the skills they seek in their workforce. For soft skills, like collaboration and critical thinking, they rarely rely on direct instruction. Instead, corporate trainers rely on simulations, team exercises and feedback to cultivate leadership skills.

Research from 2011,[122] which focused on pretest–posttest comparisons of self-efficacy, declarative knowledge, procedural knowledge, and retention in simulation games for adult workforce trainees, found that self-efficacy was significantly higher, as were declarative knowledge, procedural knowledge, and retention for trainees receiving instruction via a simulation game than for trainees in the comparison conditions. When adapted to a school context, video games provide a framework for many of the same desirable outcomes.

As pointed out in the 2018 OECD report, Teachers as Designers of Learning Environments: The Importance of Innovative Pedagogies,[123] innovative pedagogies should build on the natural learning inclinations of students. A key lever for improving the preparation of 21st century skills and the engagement of learners lies in the ability of pedagogies to match the natural inclinations of learners towards play, creativity, collaboration and inquiry.

"The fast-paced and highly engaging nature of teenagers' leisure activities often sharply contrasts with traditional classroom dynamics and teaching practices. This further contributes to declining levels of engagement. At the same time, teachers are seeking new ways to ensure that students have the knowledge and skills they need to succeed in the 21st century. Introducing play and games into classrooms, and revising teaching so that it includes elements of both, has the potential to improve student engagement and motivation, while helping equip students with new skills."[124]

In recent years there has been a growing recognition of the role that video games can play as a component in future education strategies. Gamification, or the inclusion of game-like mechanics in learning, has already become widely adopted, but the use of actual games has now been proven to support children in acquiring teamwork, tactical thinking and problem-solving skills.

In addition to the skills that can be developed through gaming, there is the further benefit that the gaming sector has been identified as a key growth segment - so exposure to the world of gaming in a structured environment can prepare students for one of the many careers associated with gaming, from game developer to professional player, shoutcaster, event organiser or commercial roles.

EStars offers internationally-accredited BTEC-level courses in esports, as well as providing its globally unique Teacher Training Framework that empowers schools to easily add gaming to their curriculum.

A systematic review and meta-analysis[125] reported overall positive effects of games as a means to enhance student learning: "Results from media comparisons indicated that digital games significantly enhanced student learning relative to nongame conditions", which aligned with a previous meta-analysis that concluded "that games and simulations led to higher cognitive outcomes and attitudinal outcomes than traditional instruction."[126]

From a pedagogical perspective, games typically offer several useful components - immediate feedback, achievement tracking, progressive difficulty, the opportunity to repeat, and a safe environment for learning.

Building on the work of Tulloch,[127] gamification should be understood as a way to implement innovative pedagogical approaches such as formative assessment, experiential learning, adaptive teaching, narrative pedagogies and collaborative learning, while focusing on the meaningful participation of all students. From this perspective, gamified teaching is not just an end in and of itself; but rather, it should be used to aid the implementation of active, student-centred, collaborative learning. As we move forward into tomorrow's classrooms, gamification can help increase student engagement and thus stimulate even better student outcomes.[128]

Metacognition

"Above all, the most basic message is that teachers and students must avoid interpreting current performance as learning"

Robert Bjork[129]

At EStars, we're big believers in the importance of learning how to learn. Being able to adapt to rapidly changing requirements is arguably the most important skill we can develop to survive and thrive in the face of uncertainty. Historically, there has been a focus in education on measurable results as the sole sign of success. However, knowledge is increasingly transient, and a more significant prize is the ability to unlearn and relearn, and to recognise when this is necessary.

The varied learning experiences that are possible in the ESCotF will be more effective where students are encouraged and equipped to reflect on their progress. In a 2008 research paper,[130]Dutch lecturer Dr. Marcel Veenman found that people who apply metacognition (evaluating how one thinks and learns) to their endeavours outscore people who have higher IQ scores - the research shows metacognition accounts for 15% points more than innate intelligence. As discussed in the book Unlock Your Learning[131],thinking about learning, planning learning and awareness of learning progress are crucial metacognition themes. We believe that such practices should be included to support whatever pedagogies are chosen. Students learn more efficiently and sustain motivation to persevere through setbacks when they understand and use strategies that brought them prior success[132].

An example that can enhance learning, from the world of metacognition, is the concept of Judgments of Learning (JoL). Unfortunately, many education situations focus on short term measures despite the fact that we humans are very bad at assessing how well we've actually learned something - that is, predicting how likely we will be to remember a piece of information or perform a skill to a given level at a later time - what academics called metamemory predictions or judgments of learning (JOL). Given that these JOLs are used to control further learning attention, our errors in judgement can lead to poor choices in our further learning: "the accuracy of JOLs is critical, because if the JOLs are inaccurate, the allocation of subsequent study time will correspondingly be less than optimal"[133]. To add to your acronyms collection, there's another concept in this space called Feeling of Knowing (FoK)[134], which describes that sense that we know we know something but can't quite recall it. We're convinced that we have learned the information and will be able to remember it and may even be able to recall it partially. Our brain has a remarkable ability to know if we've previously learned something or not, even if we can't retrieve it easily.

Fluency Falsehood

We typically base our JOLs on our confidence at a given moment in time. Reading material a second time gives a sense of fluency that should not be confused with understanding and/or long term storage. Being able to recognise information is not the same as being able to recall it unaided. Testing too soon after consuming information is not a reliable indicator of actual learning - people dramatically underpredict their own rate of forgetting. Where learners interpret current performance as a reliable measure of learning, they become susceptible to misconstruing the extent and durability of their learning.

Other important concepts include the emergence of 'cognitive load theory' which recognises that students can only take on board a certain amount of new information at a time. In the room, we have chosen some of the technologies cognisant of the work of Ericsson et al[135] on the role that deliberate practice plays in developing mastery - a single experiential learning experience may not be sufficient to develop competencies.

We recommend that teaching in the ESCotF embraces the benefits of metacognitive approaches and leverages the flexibility of the space to remind students to reflect not only on their learnings, but their retention and ability to recall/apply them. The multi-purpose nature of the room is ideal to implement recommended strategies such as interleaving and spaced repetition, allowing schools to revisit important concepts repeatedly throughout the term.

Teachers of the Future

"Statistically speaking, high-quality teachers are the strongest influence on learner achievement."

Cynthia Luna Scott[136]

Amidst all the discussion about the potential of improved learning spaces, innovative learning methodologies and new technologies to transform the learning experience for better outcomes, it's vital not to lose sight of the critical role of teachers in the delivery of the desired educational improvements. As education and technology become more deeply entwined, teaching remains a deeply human activity that should be augmented by technology rather than defined by it.

At the heart of our planning to create better classrooms for the future, we repeatedly sense check our designs to ensure everything we do is rooted in the ultimate aim of enabling teachers and students to achieve better outcomes. The ESCotF philosophy is that the technology should be a silent partner in the classroom, invisibly powering great learning experiences. Teachers must be able to harness the capabilities of the room seamlessly to amplify their teaching and be part of the technology design decisions.

Simply imposing technology in classrooms is not a viable strategy. There is a salutary reminder of the importance of involving teachers in the technology, from research such as that conducted in Norway in 2017[137] which notes "that in order to change practice it is not enough to put technology into the classroom".

As teachers consider pedagogical alternatives, they'll see the research data is replete with competing statements claiming the superiority of one teaching method over another. Our view is that there is unlikely to be one 'best' approach that is universally applicable. Instead, we encourage teachers to consider a variety of approaches and adapt contextually effective elements of each, facilitated by a flexible learning space with supporting technologies. The people charged with implementing these new teaching methods are, of course, the teachers. They should be involved at every step of the way in a constructive atmosphere to select, implement, review and refine any new methods.

Teach Better, Not Harder

*Teaching now is more dynamic, challenging and demanding than ever before. Teachers are expected to continuously innovate, adapt and develop their teaching practices to equip all students with the skills and knowledge they will need to succeed in life and work. Moreover, technological changes and the increased availability of digital resources are opening new avenues for both teaching and learning....*The only way to shorten that pipeline is for teachers themselves to be involved in the design of curricula and pedagogies, to enact and enable 21st century learning.

OECD[138]

Our education systems will have more asked of them in the coming years than at any time since their inception. The frontline teaching staff will be tasked with adapting their roles from that of information providers to facilitators of active learning, enabling students to master a wide range of knowledge and skills. Technology will be required to take on as many routine and administrative tasks as possible to free teachers to focus on higher value tasks.

In a world where access to facts is almost entirely technology-mediated, teachers will be required to oversee the development of an additional array of skills in their students. In order to succeed in the future, children must be taught to apply creativity, critical thinking and communication/collaboration competencies. As we've outlined above, this will only be possible with new facilities, pedagogies and technologies, all 'wrangled' by skilled teachers at the frontlines of the classroom.

The OECD Teaching and Learning International Survey (TALIS) and Programme for International Student Assessment (PISA) findings consistently show that student-oriented teaching strategies which place the student at the centre of the activity and give learners a more active role in lessons than in traditional teacher-directed strategies, have particularly positive effects on student learning and motivation[139]. Achieving this at scale will require both a widening of teachers' skills and a deepening of investment in supporting facilities and technologies.

Studies have concluded that impactful teachers are those who consistently achieve three central tasks: classroom management (structure); classroom climate (support); and cognitive activation (engagement and challenge)[140]. The ESCotF is designed to facilitate each of these attributes.

The Super-Teacher

The ESCotF concept is student-centric but remains teacher-dependent. Active learning emphasises the importance of involving students in their learning and letting them take ownership and responsibility, but the guidance ultimately remains within the purview of the teacher.

Teaching and learning researchers have highlighted the continuing importance of the quality of interactions between teachers and students, regardless of the environment[141]. A good teacher will spark curiosity and engagement in their students, leading to deeper learning. Teachers of the future will be super-charged by technology, but their real super-powers will be their personal ability to harness the right pedagogies and guide their students to achieve success.

When students are comfortable with the instructor, they are more comfortable learning, participating, and sharing in the learning environment. A meta-analysis of research has found a strong link between instructor warmth & empathy and student success[142].

In a report for UNESCO,[143] Cynthia Luna Scott noted that, if the main goal of twenty-first century education is to build the learning capacity of individuals and support their development into lifelong, active, independent learners, then teachers need to become 'learning coaches' – a role very different from that of a traditional classroom teacher. Teachers as learning coaches will encourage students to interact with knowledge – to understand, critique, manipulate, design, create and transform it. Or as Tawil summarised in 2013,[144] Teachers' roles will evolve from being 'dispensers of information and knowledge' to becoming 'facilitators and enablers of learning'.

To deliver on the tremendous expectations of the education sector into the future, teachers will require both enhanced classrooms and substantive continuous professional development. Just as we're advocating significant change in where and how students are taught, we must also ensure teachers have a classroom environment optimised for them to deliver educational outcomes aligned with the new paradigm of future needs, as well as revamped teacher training programmes focused on truly combining the physical and pedagogical potentials.

Pedagogical innovation must equip learners with the skills and competencies to function in a digital culture, using media and informal pathways to enrich their learning and develop essential forms of literacy. Teachers will require meaningful support and time to exploit available resources and tools to create tailor-made learning experiences that are motivating and engaging, yet efficient, relevant and challenging.

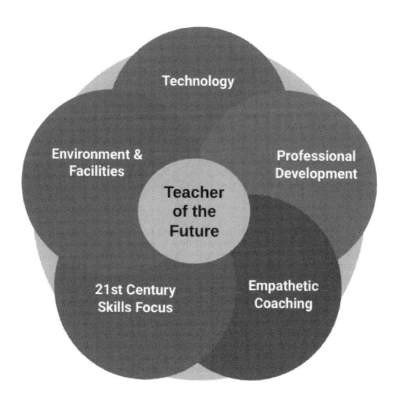

Figure: The Teacher of the Future remains at the heart of a very different school system

Universal Design for Learning (UDL)

Before we finish this section on teaching methods and move on to look at the 'what' and 'why' of teaching, let's briefly mention another important input into EStars' approach to the creation of teaching practices for the future: Universal Design for Learning, UDL.

UDL is a paradigm that prioritises inclusivity and accessibility. It promotes inherent flexibility to address the needs of all pupils, regardless of their background, abilities or any challenges or disabilities.

In short, it seeks to extend educational opportunities equally to everyone and anyone. Universal Design for Learning refers to a set of principles that provide a framework to help ensure education experiences are designed to accommodate individual learning differences. It provides teachers with a structure to develop instruction to meet the diverse needs of all learners, looking to eliminate barriers to education from the outset of the design process, rather than retrofitting solutions.

UDL has its origins in the world of architecture and product development, but was extended to the education domain by David H. Rose Researchers at the Harvard Graduate School of Education and the Center for Applied and Specialized Technologies (CAST)[145], through their efforts to integrate the work of leading educational thinkers such as Piaget, Vygotsky and Bloom.

UDL is built on three principles and outlines the needs for multiple means of:

- Engagement
- Representation
- Action & Expression

to ensure learners have a variety of ways to acquire knowledge and alternative ways to demonstrate their competence, as well as providing multiple forms of motivation.

Just as UDL advises that curricula must be designed from the outset to accommodate all types of learners, the ESCotF sets out to be accessible to all learners with this approach incorporated into all design decisions. We mandate the use of ramps or elevators for physical access and have specific assistive technologies available.

The Role of AI in Teaching

There's a cliche often used by analysts and futurists when talking about AI - *"AI won't replace teachers, but teachers who use AI will replace those who don't"*. Although still in its early phases, AI will soon rapidly pervade education, bringing both promise and peril. In this project, we're focused on the evolution and optimization of the physical classroom, but remain mindful of the impending tsunami of pedagogical innovations driven by AI.

The ESCotF is ready to support AI-powered experiments as the technology matures. We are keeping a watching brief on the space, monitoring AI-Edtech developments and contributing to the nascent measures to regulate the use of AI with particular regard to education.

We have no doubt that AI will be used extensively at every stage of the education process, from content creation (both by teachers and students) through to assessment. As it matures, it will enable breakthrough conversational and fully personalised learning experiences.

Part 3: Lessons For The Future

Having talked about optimising the physical space (Part 1), and applying evidence-based innovative pedagogies (Part 2), the final part of this book will explore the remaining key concerns of the project - the what and the why of the teaching and learning we believe will take place in the classroom of the future.

A major part of the motivation for creating the classroom of the future is the recognition that we urgently need to update the skills and competencies we equip our children with so that they are ready to thrive in the rapidly changing world they will graduate into. The education system must adapt to the changing needs of the labour market and employer expectations.

The role technology will play in the years ahead will perhaps bring about the most profound era of change yet to face humanity. Educators with a strategic vision have recognised the need for change. Saudi Arabia's Vision2030[146] commits to preparing *"a modern curriculum focused on rigorous standards in literacy, numeracy, skills and character development."* ESCotF provides the ideal setting for the delivery of this future-looking curriculum.

A Moving Target

The ESCotF was conceived with inputs from academics, curriculum planners, futurists and industry partners to identify the topics and skills that will be required in future workplaces and to help develop global citizens to their full potential.

Future graduates will need a mix of cognitive, motivational and social-based skills. They will need to be agile and able to adapt to changing realities, able to unlearn and relearn, as they go, on a lifelong basis. In a 2021 McKinsey report[147] *Adaptability* was highlighted as a key foundational skill citizens will need in the future world of work. They will also need to be able to work collaboratively and creatively and will need to be supremely comfortable with harnessing technology. And they will need to be mindful of their impact on the environment.

Acquiring this broad range of skills and knowledge will require learning spaces equipped with a mixture of technologies and facilities that address both the technical prowess and soft skills acquisition - in short, these objectives need the Classroom of the Future.

Tradition & Well-being

Despite the imperative to extend curricula to address new technologies and valuable skills, there will, of course, continue to be an important emphasis on students' acquisition of knowledge of traditional subjects. But an exciting opportunity exists there too to examine how we can enhance the teaching of these traditional subjects, making them more engaging and empowering.

The final piece of the puzzle will be to ensure that, as we prepare students for academic excellence, we also ensure they can develop their whole selves to become healthy contributors to society. The ESCotF encourages students not only to reach their full potential academically, but also to align with Vision2030's goal of creating a vibrant society, with fulfilling lives built on the happiness and fulfilment of citizens and residents, achieved through promoting physical, psychological and social well-being. To this end, the ESCotF provides the healthy environment we discussed in Part 1, but also features sustainability and facilities for students to relax.

Teaching Targets

Any new curriculum looking to the future will need to have substantially increased technology elements, along with a renewed emphasis on soft skills development. The approach will need to be firmly grounded in learning science and its success will be judged on the ability to teach students durable skills such as critical and creative thinking, emotional intelligence and sustainable innovation. The aim must be to future-proof students, not by giving them a static knowledge base, but by helping them become creative, highly effective, flexible learners who can transfer the theories and skills learnt in school into applied workplace contexts.

As we created the ESCotF, we were acutely aware of the need for the room to support the melding of teaching methods with facilities aligned with emerging workforce requirements. In Part 2, we discussed alternative teaching methods we envisage being used in ESCotF but it's worth reiterating here the widely perceived shortcomings of the current approaches when viewed with the lens of future requirements. The World Economic Forum, [148] for example, has identified four reasons why the most popular and prevalent educational model (direct instruction plus high-stakes exams) fails to meet the needs of the future:

- Lectures are one-directional knowledge pipelines which require students to passively consume information rather than actively operate on it. Research suggests, time and again, that passive learning is sub-optimal learning, leading to poorer educational outcomes compared to other (active learning) methods.
- Knowledge transmitted via lectures frequently lags behind rapid advancements in technology, industry trends and professional requirements. Consequently, many graduates enter the job market equipped with "perishable" skills ill-matched to employer needs and demands.
- High-stakes assessments (essays, exams) only capture a single moment in a student's academic journey, offering retroactive insight but little actionable feedback.
- They also tend to assess the wrong types of skills (memorization and recall) and do so under artificial conditions that rarely mimic real-world scenarios, where collaborative problem-solving and open-resource solutions are commonplace.

Skills for the Future

As we mentioned in the previous section, learning to learn will be a key skill in the years ahead. Such is the pace of innovation that whatever specific skills we teach in the classroom will likely be out of date in a short time frame. We've designed the ESCotF as a place where one can practise acquiring skills as a skill in itself. The experiential, immersive learning space encourages students to become familiar with experimentation-led, hands-on learning in a safe environment.

Among the skills we expect to see taught and learned in the classroom of the future are:

Skills	ESCotF Support
Analytical Thinking, Problem Solving	Inquiry-based Learning, Experiential Technologies, ESports
Lifelong Learning	Cognitive Psychology Principles, Advanced Technologies
Communication & Creativity	AV technologies, ESports
Digital & Technology Literacy	Robotics
Metaverse/Industrial Metaverse	Immersive Technologies, Robotics, Holography
Interpersonal Skills	Collaborative Layouts, ESports
Well-being	Meditation and Relaxation, Environmental Awareness
Cultural Appreciation	Immersive Technologies

Next Industrial Revolution Subjects

It is hopefully obvious from the table and comments herein that, while the next Industrial Revolution continues to change the way we work, we believe that soft skills – such as creativity, emotional intelligence, and critical thinking – will be more important than ever in the future of work.

Trying to predict the skills necessary for the workplace and economy of the future is not easy. The World Economic Forum's Future of Work[149] *Summary* Report runs to 296 pages! The bi-annual report tracks the labour-market impact of the next Industrial Revolution, identifying the potential scale of occupational disruption and growth alongside strategies for empowering job transitions from declining to emerging roles. The 2023 study highlights the importance of technology and green transitions, and also the importance of developing creative thinking skills - all of which are strongly reflected in the focus of the ESCotF.

Technology Showcase

This section describes the technologies we've included in the ESCotF@MGF to help prepare the classroom to teach the skills of the future. The technologies range from ones that are readily available today and likely affordable for many schools, to ones that are currently less practical and/or less affordable for mainstream use. However, we include them here to show the direction of travel in the education sector and because we believe it is important that the room be equipped with advanced technologies likely to be increasingly common in the workplaces of the future.

Note: By necessity, we've chosen specific products to display. However, the inclusion of any product should not be construed as an endorsement of suitability by EStars beyond the scope of this project. Due to the

rapidly changing technology ecosystem, schools should always consult
an appropriate expert before making any purchase decisions.

From an educational point of view, we have also chosen the
technologies to include based on a philosophy of progression. Where
possible, we have supplied basic, intermediate and advanced examples
of technologies. This is a pedagogically sound principle to support
different age groups and different learning cadence as well as providing
a clear path for students where they can see their progress and aspire
to complete each level while moving ahead with their learning.

Virtual Reality (VR) Zone

In the field of education and training, Virtual Reality has found one of its
first more effective applications. In VR, students can experience
captivating learning environments, far beyond anything that can be
achieved in a more traditional approach. VR can convincingly simulate a
vast array of scenarios, transporting students to simulated settings that
are inaccessible, dangerous or otherwise impractical in real life.

Early research on the benefits of VR in education is showing both
student preference for it and improved learning outcomes[150]. The
ESCotF has loaded the VR headsets with applications covering scientific
labs, architecture and collaboration. We predict that VR will become a
standard part of educators' toolsets in the years ahead - students will
undoubtedly use the technology in certain domains where it will add
educational value.

Headsets

For the ESCotF@MGF we are using the brand-new Meta Quest 3
headsets to demonstrate the improving capabilities of VR headsets at
the entry-level price point. These headsets offer substantial
improvements over previous generations, with 2x the processing power
and 10x the passthrough performance (which offers enhanced mixed

reality experiences). As standalone devices, these are suitable for classroom use as they don't require to be tethered to a powerful PC as was the case with earlier generations of headsets.

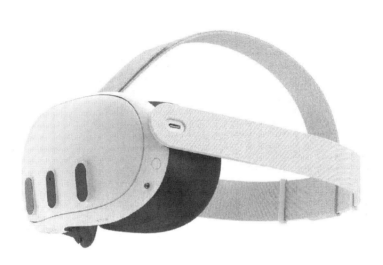

Figure: The Meta Quest 3 VR Headset

Compared to the Meta Quest Pro headsets, the Quest 3 is about half the price and offers better functionality for educational applications of VR. The Quest Pro is more focused on workplace uses due to its inward-looking face tracking cameras that enable replication of facial movements on avatars. This is not currently of significant general educational benefit, though we expect such functionality to filter down from the flagship headset price point to the more affordable models. At that point, there may be additional educational uses, particularly for students joining a class remotely.

Figure: A laboratory simulation in Virtual Reality

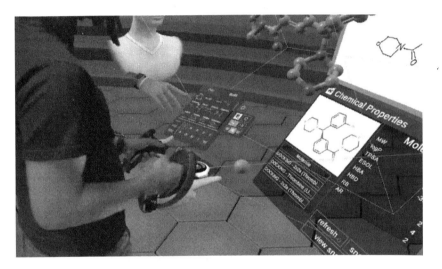

Figure: A molecular chemistry VR application

VR Treadmill

Although VR headsets offer significant educational benefits, they are an inherently static experience, where users interact primarily via hand controllers but don't physically move around - movement in the virtual setting is typically by means of 'teleportation' - point to the place in the virtual world to which you wish to move. This can reduce the sense of realism and immersion.

The ESCotF@MGF features a VR treadmill that enables students to walk (or even run) around a virtual environment in a wholly convincing manner. This emerging technology gives us a glimpse of just how immersive future VR experiences will become, as we move beyond room-scale limitations. While still early and not yet supported in a wide range of software, we expect to see a lot more VR titles add support for this experience. Growing numbers of VR treadmills are expected to come to market in 2024 and beyond.

The example treadmill experience in ESCotF@MGF is a KAT Core model, featuring height-adaptive back support for all vertical actions from jumping to crouching. As treadmill technology matures, there will be an array of industrial training scenarios that will be enhanced by the use of this technology. We believe learners will soon be able to train in virtual workplaces where motion during training is required but not currently possible.

Figure: VR Treadmill

For situations where a Treadmill is unsuitable, we're also tracking the development of in-place motion sensors for VR, such as the Kat Loco S. These collections of 3 small wearable sensors on straps allow for Walk-On-Spot locomotion enabling the user to freely walk or run on the spotin VR games.

Figure: Walk-in-place motion trackers for VR

VR Gloves

For the ultimate VR experience, the technology is evolving to bring advanced full-body experiences to fruition. Areas of research at the moment include haptic body suits that simulate collision/impact forces (popular in combat games) and a variety of haptic gloves that simulate touch. This is an important area of development to bring realism to VR experiences not possible with the current controller-centric interfaces. Even the recent advances in hand tracking, accurately replicating finger-level movement in VR, don'tdeliver the actual tactile sensationsthat would further the immersive effect.

To illustrate this exciting line of development, we've included a Weart glove that can enable lifelike interaction in VR with comprehensive haptic feedback, including force, textures, and temperature sensations. It features precise sensors to track hand and finger movements, enabling natural interactions with virtual elements and surroundings. With this technology, not only does the VR trick your brain into believing you're in a different setting, but the glove convinces your sense of touch into believing you're actually touching 'real' items.

Currently the glove technologies are somewhat immature - they are cumbersome and impractically expensive for most education settings. But as they are developed from industrial applications, they will certainly reach the realm of consumer affordability and functionality.

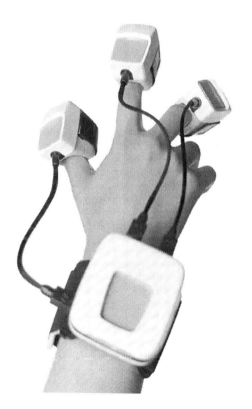

Figure: Haptic Sensors for VR that offer thermal sensation

One manufacturer has announced a less expensive haptic glove for release in 2024 but it doesn't offer thermal sensation - just haptic feedback via microfluidic actuators on the fingers and palm that mimic the sensation of touching items. It does however require a backpack sized support unit.

Among the other developments to watch in haptics will be controllers such as prototypes unveiled by Sony that can shift their internal weight to mimic holding different objects[151]. Based on the current technology trajectory, much smaller but still functional and affordable haptic solutions will be more widely available to students in a few years.

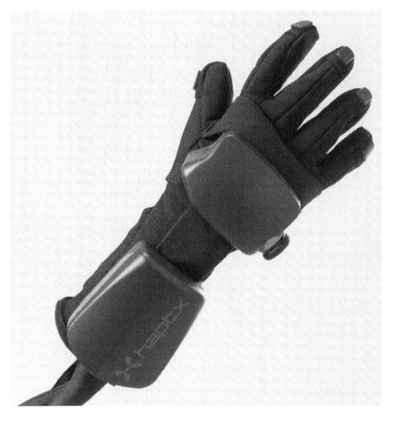

Figure: The Haptx glove (not available at time of writing)

Robotics Zone

Students of the future will likely share their world with all manner of robots. Although not yet in widespread public use, the number of robots in specialist and industrial settings is growing rapidly as the technology evolves. In particular, the growing automation of manufacturing offers large scale potential for human employment in the creation and oversight of advanced robotic solutions.

The other increasingly common types of robots that children will encounter as they grow include drone deliveries, sidewalk delivery robots, domestic single-task robots (e.g. vacuum cleaners and lawnmowers) as well as the anticipated arrival of self-driving trucks, cars and service vehicles. There has also been a notable amount of progress in the development of humanoid robots in the last 3 years and it is likely that bipedal (humanoid) robots will come to the market in the not-too-distant future.

Today's school children will need to be introduced to tomorrow's robot technologies, including the advent of fully autonomous robots. Exposure to robotics not only teaches technology and coding in a compelling and practical manner, but also reinforces computational thinking and problem-solving skills. We've equipped the ESCotF with a range of robots to introduce children to the variety of size, shapes and applications of robotics that already exist. We recommend that, to ensure relevance, robotics curricula should include coverage of larger-scale robots and applied industrial solutions from leading firms such as Boston Dynamics and Knightscope

iRobot

The first robot we have in the ESCotF@MGF is the iRobot Root. This small device is an entry level robot designed to help younger children take their first steps in learning about robotics and coding. Children can code their Root robot to draw artwork, play music, respond to touch, light, and sound, and more, all while exploring the fundamentals of robotics. As the children learn, they can progress through a fully graphical coding interface, through a hybrid interface to a more capable but complex text-driven coding interface. iRobot provide a full coding environment online to ensure students complete an approachable robotics learning experience - https://code.irobot.com/

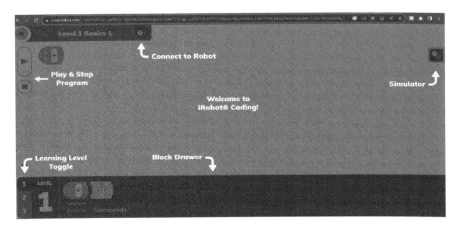

Figure - iRobot's Graphical Coding Interface

Figure: iRobot Root Device

Nao Robot

The step-up robot experience we've chosen for the ESCotF@MGF is the Nao. This small (58cm tall) humanoid-shaped robot is a proven part of many higher education robotics courses. However, we believe that older high-school students (15+) would benefit from access to such an advanced model.

This complex device has 25 degrees of freedom, 7 touch sensors located on the head, hands and feet, sonars and an inertial unit to perceive its environment and locate itself in space. In terms of human-robot interactions (HRI), it has 4 directional microphones and speakers to interact with humans in any of 20 languages, including Arabic. It also has two cameras to identify people and objects.

Although a very sophisticated device, the fact that NAO is a small humanoid device means that children can relate to it very easily. Working with NAO helps students in acquiring cross-disciplinary skills like teamwork, scientific reasoning and problem solving. Because physical devices in teaching are fundamental - students respond well to physically and visually experiencing what they are learning - NAO provides excellent and immediate feedback. Students are able to assimilate and learn when working with NAO, as they can see their work come to fruition, which builds their confidence and their newly acquired skills.

Thanks to the NAO's heritage as an educational robot, there is an array of materials available to ease its integration into the classroom. The manufacturers offer two free ebooks to help students and teachers learn quickly about robotics - https://www.aldebaran.com/en/nao-robot-education-ebook

Figure: The NAO Educational Robot

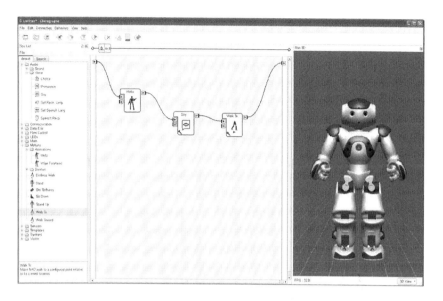

Figure - The NAO programming interface

Cobot

The final robot we have at ESCotF@MGF is an example of a cobot, or a cooperative robot. This is a miniature equivalent of an industrial robot. This 6 axis desktop robotic arm will enable students to learn a variety of technology skills including open-source hardware and software components such as Raspberry Pi 4, Python and Arduino that are already widely used in education. The robot is supported by a full learning curriculum: https://niryo.com/academy/ covering robotics, kinematics and simulation, ensuring that students can acquire a deep understanding of robotics.

The cobot offers students a progressive experience where they can start to engage with hundreds of scenarios, from simple pick-and-place tasks to complete industrial production lines. This robot also supports the concept of simulated robotics - where students can experiment with a virtual robot and then see how it applies to a real robot. This is a useful introduction to the concepts of digital twins and the increasing use of the industrial metaverse to plan factory layouts.

In an example of how agile industries in the future will leverage not only automation but additive manufacturing and rapid prototyping, the cobot's grippers can be replaced by 3D-printed variants, meaning students can try to design their own gripper jaws. As well see below, the ESCotF also includes 3D-printers, which will enable students to conceive, prototype and test new gripper designs in a practical learning assignment.

Figure: A cobot desktop robotic arm

3D-MakerZone

We talked in the previous sections of the book about the importance of experiential, hands-on learning where students are active participants and co-owners of their learning. One way that technology can support this objective is in what we call the maker-zone. This refers to technologies that allow students to create physical objects - tactile learning exercises that ensure a balanced range of skills alongside the virtual and screen-based curriculum components. While we're focused on tangible learning experiences, we're also aware of the blurring lines between physical and digital realities so we will also look at creation of 3D virtual objects that will exist in digital form in the metaverse.

Making More of Making

Traditional school classes have largely favoured theoretical and academic subjects over activities where physical items are created or produced. However, thanks to new technologies that enable creative endeavours without heavy equipment (such as that required for woodwork or metalwork classes) and a growing recognition of the broader educational benefits of such activities, it's now possible to incorporate a range of 'maker' modules into the Classroom of the Future.

Research[152] into the value and potential of 'making' as an educational tool confirms that it promotes qualities such as problem solving, design thinking, collaboration and innovation. However, studies to date have noted the field remains new and current research on making is largely focused on describing the phenomenon in the form of case studies, or on discussing societal and technological developments, rather than focusing on learners' experience and how to enable engaging and joyful learning. There is, therefore, a need to provide insights on how making can help us to advance current learning practices. Technologies to enable making in a classroom align with Constructionism and "learning-by-making" principles[153] that espouse discovery of knowledge as preferable to just receiving it passively.

Students graduating from ESCotF classrooms will enter a world where rapid prototyping is commonplace and creating 3D objects is easy. To ensure they are equipped with a foundational understanding of this domain, we've created space in the ESCotF to experiment hands-on with the latest 3D technologies.

3D printers are a fascinating technology for students as they see 3D models, created on screen, come to life in the classroom. We've chosen a high speed, wi-fi enabled, enclosed printer that can be remote controlled and monitored via a built-in camera. Conscious of the lengthy printing times that might not suit lesson times, the unit is quiet enough to be left working without disturbing the class (remember back to our discussion of background noise!). The 3D printer is easy to use and is up to 10 times faster than legacy models. It includes one-button levelling and diagnostics, with a display to ensure students and teachers are fully aware at all times of what's going on.

Figure: 3D Printer

Students can also create 3D models of physical items using the special 3D scanning camera, manipulate the resulting model and then output it as a 3D printed item. The 3D scanner offers high precision scanning with accuracy up to 0.1 mm, capturing high resolution full-colour textures for creating 3D models. Teachers and students can compare and contrast 3D scanning with the latest Lidar, NeRF and Gaussian-splatting-powered scanning and rendering techniques, inline with what we believe will be an increasing emphasis on 3D objects in the years ahead.

Figure: 3D Scanner

We've also included a laser engraver to show students how lasers can be applied in industrial contexts, for example to personalise products. As another type of technology that students may encounter in the workplace, the engraver is safe, easy to use and can work on a variety of surfaces.

Figure: Laser Engraver

Holography

"By modeling instructional content and behavior in relatable contexts, holographic characters, tools and visuals can uniquely motivate students and promote interactive engagement in learning activities"

Robin A Walker[154]

In the ESCotF, we are looking for ways to bring learning to life. Holograms are an exciting technology with real potential to improve educational access and engagement. As a technology, 3D holograms have retained a very science-fiction vibe, crucially different from VR or Augmented Reality/Mixed Reality (AR/MR), in that they don't require a headset or glasses (head-mounted display - HMD) but are visible to the naked eye.

Although technically challenging to implement, developments in the underlying techniques involved in creating holograms mean they are becoming more affordable and available. This trend should be of particular interest to educators, given their suitability for education and significant advantages over 'flat' media.

Compared to a static 2D-image, advancements in holography can bring complex concepts to life in new ways. In a classroom, students can gather around a 3D hologram but still have full presence with their classmates and teachers, which isn't possible using HMD technologies. In subjects such as biology, physics or chemistry, where students need to visualise abstract concepts, holograms can be particularly helpful to show realistic, interactive representations of topics. Holograms can combine the 3D 'walk-around' nature of a physical prop with the digital capabilities to zoom/explode or demonstrate movement.

Holograms can also be used to add depth to interactions with remote experts. So, instead of having someone join the class in a standard Zoom call, holograms can be used to give a real sense of presence.

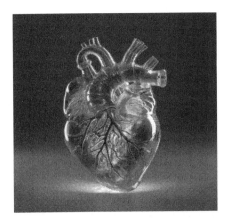
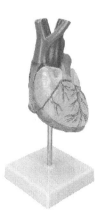

Figure: A holographic teaching aid (L) can show motion/transparency unlike a static model (R)

ESCotF@MGF has two holograms, one of which is a central unit that features prominently in the class, intended to display educational content such as anatomical models that the students can gather around. This device, the Dreamoc XXL3, offers students a clear and vivid view of the hologram in 4K or full HD video - which is hugely engaging.

And building on the ethos of our 3D-Maker Zone, the presence of the display hologram will act as an additional 3D canvas. Students will be able to create their own holographic content for display on the main hologram unit in the ESCotF, offering unprecedented opportunities for skills development.

Figure: The Large Display Hologram

So that students in the classroom can interact with experts from all over the world, we've also added a HoloBox, an 86" screen that can video-conference with remote locations in real time. Whether used for live special guests or pre-recorded presentations from global contributors, the students in the ESCotF can enjoy compelling educational sessions like no others. The added depth, realism and range of motions far exceed what's possible with 2D conferencing.

Figure: The Holobox

Again, we're closely monitoring the evolution of this stream of technology and we're excited by the developments that are coming into view. While the Holobox currently requires specialised equipment, newer prototypes like the Google Starline[155] project promise to bring more immersive video interactions to desktop-sized experiences. This opens up additional avenues for global connections that feel more real than current 'flat' experiences:

"Project Starline works like a magic window where you can talk, gesture and make eye contact with another person, life-size and in three dimensions. The system uses advanced AI to build a photorealistic model of the person you're talking to, and projects that onto a light field display with a unique sense of volume and depth. The result is a lifelike image of the other person as if they were right in front of you."

We expect to see this kind of technology adapted for education use in the years ahead to create immersive experiences and connect invited speakers to classrooms and students across the world.

Figure: A Google Project Starline desktop prototype

We believe that holograms, along with VR and other mixed-reality HMD technologies, offer immense opportunities to make learning more engaging. By bringing complex concepts to life in three dimensions, students can learn in a far more compelling manner, with the ability to conceptualise through interactive visualisations.

Cognitive studies have looked at how three-dimensional images in the form of holograms should be used more in teaching and learning, especially in the field of STEM. Research indicates perceptual effects on student comprehension as well as other strong educational benefits, when instruction is mediated by 3-D imagery. Findings show objects that move or undergo perspective transformations are potentially more informative than stationary objects[156].

Tech for Teachers

Throughout this project, EStars has kept front of mind the teachers - who will orchestrate the ESCotF in practice. From the control systems for the room to the individual technologies present, we've designed everything to be as simple and seamless for teachers as possible. We are adamant that the technology is there to support the teaching experience, not hinder it. Every piece of technology has a matching guide for teachers that explains not just its operation but also the educational rationale, with suggestions about how it can be integrated into practical teaching plans.

EStars built the world's first ESports Teacher Framework for the rollout of the BTEC in ESports programmes we're now known for. We've leveraged our experience and learnings from that to ensure teachers are adequately supported in their transition to ESCotF - just as their young charges need to be prepared for the future, so too the future role of teachers is changing, and current supports are not future-ready.

Figure 6: Teachers work about 50 hours a week, spending less than half the time in direct interaction with students.

Activity composition of teacher working hours, number of hours

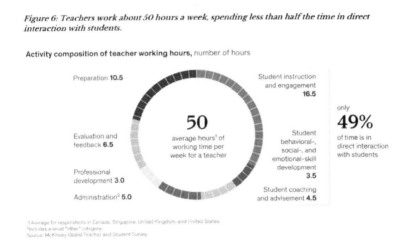

Preparation **10.5**

Student instruction and engagement **16.5**

only **49%** of time is in direct interaction with students

50 average hours[1] of working time per week for a teacher

Evaluation and feedback **6.5**

Student behavioral-, social-, and emotional-skill development **3.5**

Professional development **3.0**

Administration[2] **5.0**

Student coaching and advisement **4.5**

[1] Average for respondents in Canada, Singapore, United Kingdom, and United States.
[2] Includes a small "other" category.
Source: McKinsey Global Teacher and Student Survey

A McKinsey report on the impact of AI on teaching has highlighted the opportunities technology offers to free up teachers to have more time to teach which, combined with more effective pedagogies, really does offer great hope for taking education to the next level.

Part 4: Room Layouts

Throughout our description of the ESCotF, we've emphasised the importance of flexibility. Just as we want the graduates of the ESCotF to be agile and adaptable, the learning space itself is flexible in sympathy with its users.

Ultimately, we're excited to see what teachers and students can achieve in the room and we know their creative minds will harness the facilities we've included in ways we never imagined.

Virtual Floorplans with Lightguides

To provide a starting point from which we encourage individual teachers and classes to build and create their own variations, we've proposed a number of predefined room layouts/modes. These layouts have been carefully tested to ensure compliance with the sorts of physical factors discussed in Part 1, e.g. each predefined layout/mode has been checked to calibrate for optimal lighting, acoustic and airflow parameters.

The room control system can indicate the appropriate locations in each mode for the relevant furniture and technology by illuminating a virtual floorplan. Teachers can save their own preferred floorplans for future use.

All of the technologies described above will follow the normal development curve of technology - they will get smaller, cheaper and better. Technology that currently requires wheels to move and takes up a significant amount of room in the class will soon be small enough to pick up and carry around. In the interim, we've created a vision for a room as flexible as contemporary technology allows and we've built in storage space to facilitate practical transitions between uses.

Direct Teaching - Stage

The direct teaching mode is the most conventional-looking layout for the ESCotF. As we said in the pedagogy section, there are still times when direct instruction is the most appropriate method and we've taken steps to ensure we provide a modern spin on this traditional approach.

The teacher takes their place at the front of the room, while students are arranged in a semicircle, with or without tables as preferred. This is to ensure maximum participation and the best lines of sight, speech intelligibility and minimal glare.

While we have defined default settings, we strongly encourage teachers and students to personalise the room to create a sense of ownership and community in the room.

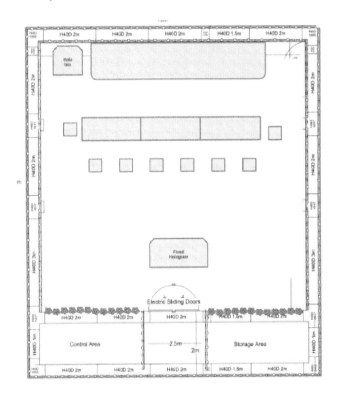

Figure: The Teaching - Stage Mode Layout

The key elements of the room are configured by default as follows:

Walls	Virtual Classroom, subject-appropriate educational posters, optional nudge mode, air quality displays, virtual windows with perspective views to reduce eyestrain.
Floor	Choice of traditional carpet, marble effect or subject-appropriate
Ceiling	Choice of virtual sky, virtual ceiling or subject-appropriate
Lighting	Optimised for desk layout
Desks	Arranged in Semi-circle
Seating	Chairs, stools as per personal preference
Display Hologram	Optional, if subject appropriate content available. Otherwise, in dim mode
Holobox	Optional, if remote guest relevant

Direct Teaching - Hologram

The direct teaching mode - hologram is for sessions where there is a substantial amount of holographic content. Students are invited to gather around the hologram while the teacher explains key concepts, or the students interact with the hologram display.

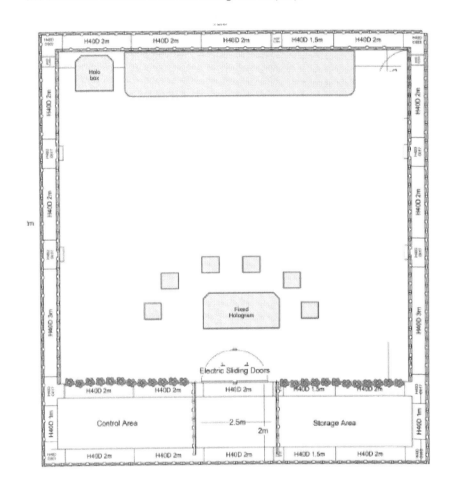

Figure: The Teaching - Hologram Mode Layout

The key elements of the room are configured by default as follows:

Walls	Subject specific content, dimmed to focus attention on holographic content
Floor	Choice of traditional carpet, marble effect or subject-appropriate
Ceiling	Virtual ceiling or subject-appropriate, dimmed to focus attention on holographic content
Desks	N/A
Seating	Stools around hologram
Display Hologram	Subject appropriate content
Holobox	N/A

Games Mode

The Games mode layout for ESCotF focuses on creating a fun environment for gaming.

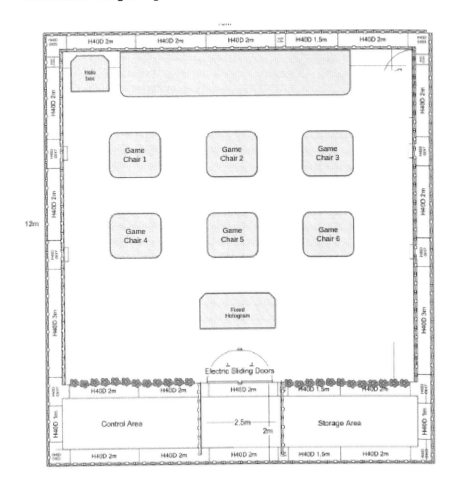

Figure: The Gaming Mode Layout

The key elements of the room are configured by default as follows:

Walls	Gaming imagery, PIP from play, Scoreboard, Shoutcaster
Floor	High-tech gaming floor with RGB effects
Ceiling	High-tech gaming ceiling with RGB effects
Desks	Gaming Pods
Seating	Gaming Pods
Display Hologram	Dimmed
Holobox	N/A

Group Collaboration Mode

The Group Collaboration Mode for ESCotF focuses on creating an active classroom environment for effective group work.

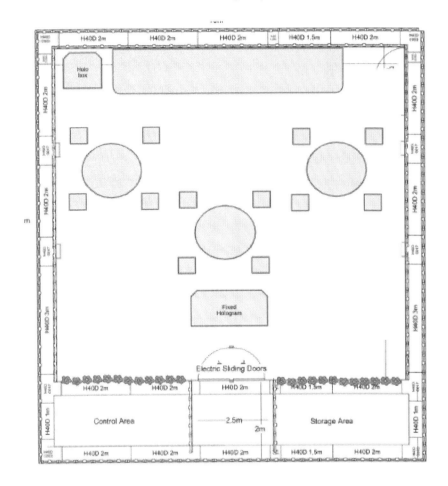

Figure: The Collaboration/Groupwork Mode Layout

The key elements of the room are configured by default as follows:

Walls	Virtual Classroom, subject-appropriate educational posters, optional nudge mode, air quality displays, virtual windows with perspective views to reduce eyestrain.
Floor	Choice of traditional carpet, marble effect or subject-appropriate
Ceiling	Choice of virtual sky, virtual ceiling or subject-appropriate
Lighting	Optimised for collaborative desk layout
Desks	Clustered
Seating	Chairs, stools as per personal preference
Display Hologram	N/A
Holobox	N/A

Nature Mode

The Nature mode layout for ESCotF focuses on creating a calm environment for relaxation, meditation or quiet solo study.

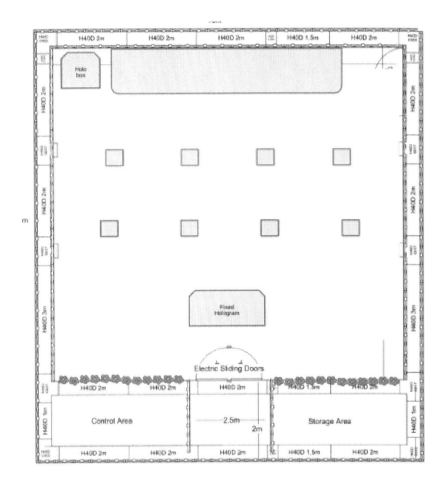

Figure: The Nature Mode Layout

The key elements of the room are configured by default as follows:

Walls	Forest Scene
Floor	Forest Floor
Ceiling	Forest Canopy/Sky
Desks	Removed
Seating	Yoga Mats or Beanbags as preferred
Display Hologram	Dimmed
Holobox	N/A
Scent	Forest Fresh Scent

Zones Mode

The Zones mode layouts for ESCotF are subject-specific modes based on the particular activities.

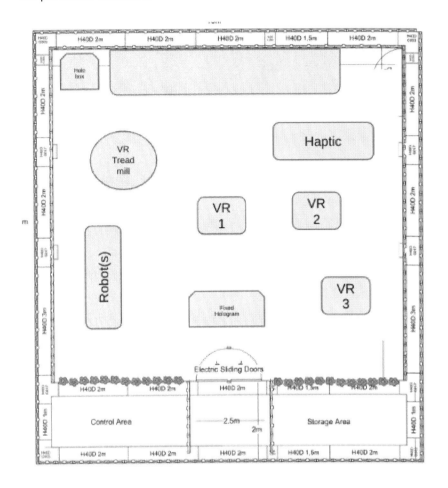

Figure: The Zones Mode Layout

The key elements of the room are configured by default as follows:

Walls	Next Industrial Revolution imagery, Metaverse
Floor	High-tech floor
Ceiling	High Tech ceiling
Desks	Tables for Technology items
Seating	Stools
Display Hologram	Dimmed
Holobox	N/A

Conclusion

Computers haven't had the effect on education that many of us in the industry have hoped. There have been some good developments....but they haven't had a meaningful effect on any of the measures of students' achievement. But I think in the next five to 10 years, AI-driven software will finally deliver on the promise of revolutionizing the way people teach and learn.

Bill Gates

Seizing the opportunity to reimagine our classrooms is a clear imperative. What we teach and how we teach it impacts virtually all walks of life and forms the foundation for much of what will be achieved in the decades ahead. Technology will take on new roles in society and force us to fundamentally rethink what's possible, what's desirable and what our vision is to be.

Implementing future-focused learning environments will quickly empower progressive schools and individuals, while laggards may fall irrecoverably behind. In the education space, the scale of impending disruption dwarfs even that of the printing press. We are about to see the biggest change in education since the emergence of the Socratic method in 400 BCE.

The Future is a Journey

We see the future as a journey, not a destination. While we can ideate about an ideal future point, it is important to find pragmatic solutions to benefit from without waiting. While technology moves at an astonishing pace, it can be foolish to wait for a perfect product. Some products may not be ready yet for widespread use, but sometimes anticipated incremental advances can delay decision-making and application in class; however, their additional benefits may be minor and inconsequential. Rather than miss the opportunity to introduce an emerging technology to classrooms, it may be preferable to show students the imperfect state and spark their imagination on how a technology might evolve.

This book sets out something of a thought-experiment and directional vision rather than a singular recommended path. The ESCotF project is the beginning of a conversion, not a prescriptive solution. It is Intended to encourage engagement, debate and experimentation. It is not presented as a completed blueprint, but a starting point that can and should be further developed, adapted and refined. We see it as a step in exploring the tremendous potential ahead, an opportunity to unlock the potential of our schoolchildren and elevate our approach to teaching to better align it with the ambitious national vision and a much-changed future.

We aim to guide educators in understanding what these emerging technologies can do to advance educational goals—while evaluating and limiting key risks. There are, of course, numerous local factors that will determine the pace and scope of classroom evolution; from demographics and space constraints to budgetary limits, individual schools and educational authorities will have to make their own decisions.

We eschew gimmicks but favour experimentation to understand how novel technologies and approaches can be combined to capture children's imagination and inspire their curiosity. It's important to point out that what we describe here is not a literal blueprint for a room, but the fusion of ingredients that can be selected locally based on numerous factors.

We view the ESCotF@MGF as a laboratory; a concept space to illustrate and demonstrate, to provoke and inspire. We thank Misk for the opportunity to share our vision and contribute to the debate about the direction and definition of how classrooms should evolve. We hope you find our vision compelling.

What's Past is Prologue

Traditionally among the more conservative of sectors, education has already struggled to embrace digital disruption and go beyond the rollout of basic technology. But these changes will soon seem like an opening act - what lies ahead will bring disruption on a scale unlike anything that's gone before.

The classroom of the future should acknowledge the reality of its students. They are unlike prior generations in terms of both their exposure to technology to date, and the technological world into which they will emerge from their schooling. AI may be grabbing the headlines but plenty of other significant technologies are coming. In isolation, each of these represents substantial change but, together, they are nothing short of a revolution.

We still have untapped breakthroughs in the understanding of effective learning techniques and more technology at our disposal than ever before. But we need to harness these to ensure we create a learning environment that truly prepares children to contribute and prosper in a society reshaped by exponential technologies, AI and sustainability concerns.

Building the classroom of the future is a great privilege but one that comes with great responsibility. The classroom of the future is an empty room until it's filled with the teachers and students that represent the future. The ESCotF team is focused on what the room can, should, and must achieve. We recognise the importance of why people are learning and what they need to learn. To do it successfully, they need classroom support very different from the historical focus of classrooms on passive, undifferentiated delivery of content. Success will be measured by the creation of a generation ready for whatever the future holds, an empowered generation ready to fulfil their potential.

At EStars, we see vast potential. We have designed a learning space that is practical, flexible and engaging. We encourage schools and teachers to embrace it. Our children *need* the best possible preparation for the future. They *deserve* the best possible preparation for the future - let's build the classroom of the future for them.

"If the children and youth of a nation are afforded opportunity to develop their capacities to the fullest, if they are given the knowledge to understand the world and the wisdom to change it, then the prospects for the future are bright."

Urie Bronfenbrenner

"Education is the passport to the future, for tomorrow belongs to those who prepare for it today."

Malcolm X

References

[1] Alejo, Anna, and Haogen Yao, "Recovering learning: Are children and youth on track in skills development?", Education Commission and UNICEF, 2022

[2] https://en.wikipedia.org/wiki/Wicked_problem

[3] Peter Barrett, Fay Davies, Yufan Zhang, Lucinda Barrett, The impact of classroom design on pupils' learning: Final results of a holistic, multi-level analysis, Building and Environment, Volume 89, 2015,

Pages 118-133, ISSN 0360-1323,
https://doi.org/10.1016/j.buildenv.2015.02.013

[4] https://en.wikipedia.org/wiki/History_of_education

[5] https://www.nybooks.com/articles/1970/07/02/why-we-must-abolish-schooling/

[6] https://mashable.com/article/future-education

[7] Hod, Y. (2017). Future Learning Spaces in Schools: Concepts and Designs from the Learning Sciences. Journal of Formative Design in Learning, 1(2), 99-109

[8]
https://services.google.com/fh/files/misc/future_of_the_classroom_emerging_trends_in_k12_education.pdf

[9] https://www.fastcompany.com/90903364/4-ways-ai-will-change-the-classroom-with-khan-academy-founder-sal-khan

[10] Clark, Ruth & Mayer, Richard & Thalheimer, Will. (2003). E-Learning and the Science of Instruction: Proven Guidelines for Consumers and Designers of Multimedia Learning. Performance Improvement. 42. 10.1002/pfi.4930420510

[11] Wolf Maryanne and C. J. Stoodley. 2018. Reader Come Home : The Reading Brain in a Digital World. First ed. New York NY: Harper an imprint of HarperCollinsPublishers

[12] Clinton, V. (2019) Reading from paper compared to screens: A systematic review and meta-analysis. Journal of Research in Reading, 42: 288–325. https://doi.org/10.1111/1467-9817.12269

[13] https://sdgs.un.org/goals/goal4

[14] https://education.minecraft.net/wp-content/uploads/13679_EDU_Thought_Leadership_Summary_revisions_5.10.18.pdf

[15] https://iste.org/standards/students

[16] https://www.oecd.org/general/thecasefor21st-centurylearning.htm

[17] Shengquan Yu, 2019

[18] European Commission A study on smart, effective, and inclusive investment in education infrastructure, 2022 PDF ISBN 978-92-76-49250-4 doi:10.2766/8576 NC-03-22-006-EN-N

[19] Tanner, C.K. (2000), "The influence of school architecture on academic achievement", Journal of Educational Administration, Vol. 38 No. 4, pp. 309-330. https://doi.org/10.1108/09578230010373598

[20] School Design, Henry Sanoff, Routledge, 1994

[21] https://finland.fi/life-society/building-an-even-better-finnish-school/

[22] ibid

[23] Tanner, C.K. (2009), "Effects of school design on student outcomes", Journal of Educational Administration, Vol. 47 No. 3, pp. 381-399. https://doi.org/10.1108/09578230910955809

[24] David, T.G. and Weinstein, CS. (1987), "The built environment and children's development, in Weinstein, CS and David, T.G. (Eds), Spaces for Children: The Built Environment and Child Development, Plenum Press, New York, NY, pp. 3-40.

[25] Kunz W.S. (1998), "Research: pictures at an exhibition", The Educational Facility Planner, Vol. 34 No. 2, pp. 5-9.

[26] Ibid

[27] https://www.a4le.org/

[28] Tanner, C.K. (2000), "The influence of school architecture on academic achievement", Journal of Educational Administration, Vol. 38 No. 4, pp. 309-330. https://doi.org/10.1108/09578230010373598

[29] Jeremy D. Finn, Academic and non-cognitive effects of small classes, International Journal of Educational Research, Volume 96, 2019, Pages 125-135, ISSN 0883-0355,

https://doi.org/10.1016/j.ijer.2019.05.006.

[30] Meek, A. and Landfried, S. (1995). Crow Island School: 54 Years Young. In A. Meek (Ed.), Designing Places for Learning (pp. 51-59.). Alexandria, VA: ASCD.

[31] Peter Barrett, Fay Davies, Yufan Zhang, Lucinda Barrett, The impact of classroom design on pupils' learning: Final results of a holistic, multi-level analysis, Building and Environment, Volume 89, 2015,

Pages 118-133, ISSN 0360-1323,
https://doi.org/10.1016/j.buildenv.2015.02.013

[32] Barrett P, Davies F, Zhang Y, Barrett L. The Holistic Impact of Classroom Spaces on Learning in Specific Subjects. Environ Behav. 2017 May;49(4):425-451. doi: 10.1177/0013916516648735. Epub 2016 May 16. PMID: 28458394; PMCID: PMC5394432

[33] https://www.edutopia.org/article/flexible-classrooms-research-scarce-promising

[34] https://www.epa.gov/coronavirus/ventilation-and-coronavirus-covid-19

[35] https://www.who.int/news-room/questions-and-answers/item/coronavirus-disease-covid-19-ventilation-and-air-conditioning

[36] David A. Coley, Rupert Greeves & Brian K. Saxby (2007) The Effect of Low Ventilation Rates on the Cognitive Function of a Primary School Class, International Journal of Ventilation, 6:2, 107-112, DOI: 10.1080/14733315.2007.11683770

[37] Bearer CF. Environmental health hazards: how children are different from adults. Future Child. 1995 Summer-Fall;5(2):11-26. PMID: 8528683

[38] Allen, Joseph G., Piers MacNaughton, Usha Satish, Suresh Santanam, Jose Vallarino, and John D. Spengler. 2015. "Associations of Cognitive Function Scores with Carbon Dioxide, Ventilation, and Volatile Organic Compound Exposures in Office Workers: A Controlled Exposure Study of Green and Conventional Office Environments." Environmental Health Perspectives 124 (6): 805-812. doi:10.1289/ehp.1510037. http://dx.doi.org/10.1289/ehp.1510037

[39] Pawel Wargocki & David P. Wyon (2007) The Effects of Moderately Raised Classroom Temperatures and Classroom Ventilation Rate on the Performance of Schoolwork by Children (RP-1257), HVAC&R Research, 13:2, 193-220, DOI: 10.1080/10789669.2007.10390951

[40] Er Ding, Dadi Zhang, Philomena M. Bluyssen, Ventilation regimes of school classrooms against airborne transmission of infectious respiratory droplets: A review, Building and Environment,

Volume 207, Part A, 2022, 108484, ISSN 0360-1323, https://doi.org/10.1016/j.buildenv.2021.108484

[41] Ventilation procedures to minimize the airborne transmission of viruses at schools

L. Stabile, A. Pacitto, A. Mikszewski, L. Morawska, G. Buonanno. medRxiv 2021.03.23.21254179; doi: https://doi.org/10.1101/2021.03.23.21254179

[42] https://www.cdc.gov/coronavirus/2019-ncov/community/schools-childcare/ventilation.html

[43] https://www.ashrae.org/technical-resources/bookstore/standards-62-1-62-2

[44] https://www.cdc.gov/coronavirus/2019-ncov/community/schools-childcare/interactive-ventilation-tool.html

[45] https://www.connectionsbyfinsa.com/the-importance-of-lighting-this-is-how-you-do-it/

[46] McColl SL, Veitch JA. Full-spectrum fluorescent lighting: a review of its effects on physiology and health. Psychol Med. 2001 Aug;31(6):949-64. doi: 10.1017/s0033291701004251. PMID: 11513381

[47] https://www.ucl.ac.uk/bartlett/environmental-design/news/2022/mar/importance-daylighting-classrooms-and-its-effect-primary-students-academic-performance

[48] Mott, M. S., Robinson, D. H., Walden, A., Burnette, J., & Rutherford, A. S. (2012). Illuminating the Effects of Dynamic Lighting on Student Learning. SAGE Open, 2(2). https://doi.org/10.1177/2158244012445585

[49] Barkmann, Claus & Wessolowski, Nino & Schulte-Markwort, Michael. (2012). Applicability and efficacy of variable light in schools. Physiology & behavior. 105. 621-7. 10.1016/j.physbeh.2011.09.020

[50] Mark Winterbottom, Arnold Wilkins; Lighting and discomfort in the classroom, Journal of Environmental Psychology, Volume 29, Issue 1, 2009, Pages 63-75, ISSN 0272-4944,

https://doi.org/10.1016/j.jenvp.2008.11.007

[51] https://www.makegreatlight.com/about-us/blog/classroom-lighting-other-creative-ways-to-enhance-student-engagement

[52] Heschong, Lisa. (1999). Daylighting in Schools An Investigation into the Relationship Between Daylighting and Human Performance Condensed Report. 10.13140/RG.2.2.31498.31683.

[53] Rikard Küller, Carin Lindsten, Health and behavior of children in classrooms with and without windows, Journal of Environmental Psychology, Volume 12, Issue 4, 1992, Pages 305-317, ISSN 0272-4944, https://doi.org/10.1016/S0272-4944(05)80079-9

[54] Mott, M. S., Robinson, D. H., Walden, A., Burnette, J., & Rutherford, A. S. (2012). Illuminating the Effects of Dynamic Lighting on Student Learning. SAGE Open, 2(2). https://doi.org/10.1177/2158244012445585

[55]

https://www.cisca.org/files/public/Acoustics%20in%20Schools%20Summary%20Flyer.pdf

[56] https://www.who.int/features/factfiles/mental_health/en/

[57] Bronzaft, A. L., & McCarthy, D. P. (1975). The effect of elevated train noise on reading ability. Environment and Behavior, 7(4), 517–527. https://doi.org/10.1177/001391657500700406

[58] Acoustical Society of America, "Position on the Use of Sound Amplification in the Classroom," undated." http://asa.aip.org/amplification.pdf

[59] Wróblewski M, Lewis DE, Valente DL, Stelmachowicz PG. Effects of reverberation on speech recognition in stationary and modulated noise by school-aged children and young adults. Ear Hear. 2012 Nov-Dec;33(6):731-44. doi: 10.1097/AUD.0b013e31825aecad. PMID: 22732772; PMCID: PMC3474865

[60] Astolfi A, Puglisi GE, Murgia S, Minelli G, Pellerey F, Prato A, Sacco T. Influence of Classroom Acoustics on Noise Disturbance and Well-Being for First Graders. Front Psychol. 2019 Dec 13;10:2736. doi: 10.3389/fpsyg.2019.02736. PMID: 31920797; PMCID: PMC6923245

[61] Jianxin Peng, Siu-Kit Lau, Yuezhe Zhao, Comparative study of acoustical indices and speech perception of students in two primary school classrooms with an acoustical treatment, Applied Acoustics, Volume 164, 2020, 107297, ISSN 0003-682X, https://doi.org/10.1016/j.apacoust.2020.107297

[62] https://webstore.ansi.org/standards/asa/ansiasas12602010partr2015

[63] Classroom Acoustics for Children with Normal Hearing and with Hearing Impairment. Carl C Crandell & Joseph J Smaldino. Language, Speech and Hearing Services in Schools, Vol. 31, p362-370 October 2000

[64] https://acoustics.org/pressroom/httpdocs/133rd/2paaa1.html

[65] Astolfi A., Bottalico P., Accornero A., Garzaro M., Nadalin J., Giordano C. (2012a). "Relationship between vocal doses and voice disorders on primary school teachers," in Proceedings of the Conference on Noise Control – EuroNoise2012, Prague

[66] Noise in open plan classrooms in primary schools: A review. Shield Bridget, Greenland Emma, Dockrell Julie. Year : 2010 | Volume: 12 | Issue Number: 49 | Page: 225-234

[67] https://www.ioa.org.uk/sites/default/files/Acoustics%20of%20Schools%20-%20a%20design%20guide%20November%202015_1.pdf

[68] Burda, J., & Brooks, C. (1996). College classroom seating position and changes in achievement motivation over a semester. Psychological Reports, 78, 331-336

[69] Fernandes, Amanda Careena, et al. "Does where a student sits really matter?--the impact of seating locations on student classroom learning." International Journal of Applied Educational Studies, vol. 10, no. 1, Apr. 2011, pp. 66+. Gale Academic OneFile, link.gale.com/apps/doc/A256070886/AONE?u=googlescholar&sid=bookmark-AONE&xid=5e827538

[70] Perkins, K., & Wieman, C. (2005). The surprising impact of seat location on student performance. The Physics Teacher, 43, 30-33

[71] Sommer, R. (1977). Classroom layout. Theory into Practice, 16(3), 174-175

[72] Marx, A., Fuhrer, U., & Hartig, T. (1999). Effects of classroom seating arrangements on children's question-asking. Learning Environments Research, 2(3), 249–263. https://doi.org/10.1023/A:1009901922191

[73] Pedro F.S. Rodrigues, Josefa N.S. Pandeirada, When visual stimulation of the surrounding environment affects children's cognitive performance, Journal of Experimental Child Psychology, Volume 176, 2018, Pages 140-149, ISSN 0022-0965, https://doi.org/10.1016/j.jecp.2018.07.014

[74] Fisher, A. V., Godwin, K. E., & Seltman, H. (2014). Visual Environment, Attention Allocation, and Learning in Young Children: When Too Much of a Good Thing May Be Bad. Psychological Science, 25(7), 1362–1370. https://doi.org/10.1177/0956797614533801

[75] Peter Barrett, Fay Davies, Yufan Zhang, Lucinda Barrett, The impact of classroom design on pupils' learning: Final results of a holistic, multi-level analysis, Building and Environment, Volume 89, 2015, Pages 118-133, ISSN 0360-1323, https://doi.org/10.1016/j.buildenv.2015.02.013

[76] https://www.edutopia.org/article/dos-and-donts-classroom-decorations

[77] Pile, John. (1997) Color in Interior Design, New York: McGraw-Hill

[78] Taylor, Anne. "The Learning Environment as a Three-Dimensional Textbook." Children's Environments, vol. 10, no. 2, 1993, pp. 170–79. JSTOR, http://www.jstor.org/stable/41514891.

[79] https://www.edutopia.org/article/flexible-classrooms-research-scarce-promising

[80] https://en.wikipedia.org/wiki/No_Child_Left_Behind_Act

[81] https://corp.kaltura.com/blog/innovative-teaching-strategies/

[82] https://www.brookings.edu/articles/approaches-to-pedagogical-innovation-and-why-they-matter/

[83] Paniagua, A. and D. Istance (2018), Teachers as Designers of Learning Environments: The Importance of Innovative Pedagogies, Educational Research and Innovation, OECD Publishing, Paris http://dx.doi.org/10.1787/9789264085374-en

[84] Dumont, H., D. Istance and F. Benavides (eds.) (2010), The Nature of Learning: Using Research to Inspire Practice, OECD Publishing, Paris, http://dx.doi.org/10.1787/9789264086487-en

[85] Pollard, A. (ed.) (2010), Professionalism as Pedagogy: A Contemporary Opportunity: A

Commentary By TLRP And GTCE, TLRP, London

[86] Innovative Pedagogies of the Future: An Evidence-Based Selection. Frontiers in Education, Vol. 4, 2019. DOI=10.3389/feduc.2019.00113

[87] https://www.sri.com/press/blog-archive/innovating-pedagogies-sri-education-and-uks-open-university-uncover-ten-trends/

[88] Åsa Hirsh, Claes Nilholm, Henrik Roman, Eva Forsberg & Daniel Sundberg (2022) Reviews of teaching methods – which fundamental issues are identified?, Education Inquiry, 13:1, 1-20, DOI: 10.1080/20004508.2020.1839232

[89] OECD (2018), Teaching for the Future: Effective Classroom Practices To Transform Education, OECD Publishing, Paris, https://doi.org/10.1787/9789264293243-en

[90] Bonwell, C. C., & Eison, J. A. (1991). Active Learning: Creating Excitement in the Classroom. ASHE-ERIC Higher Education Report, Washington DC: School of Education and Human Development, George Washington University

[91] Freeman S, Eddy SL, McDonough M, Smith MK, Okoroafor N, Jordt H, Wenderoth MP. Active learning increases student performance in science, engineering, and mathematics. Proc Natl Acad Sci U S A. 2014 Jun 10;111(23):8410-5. doi: 10.1073/pnas.1319030111. Epub 2014 May 12. PMID: 24821756; PMCID: PMC4060654.

[92] Deslauriers, Louis & McCarty, Logan & Miller, Kelly & Callaghan, Kristina & Kestin, Greg. (2019). Measuring actual learning versus feeling of learning in response to being actively engaged in the classroom. Proceedings of the National Academy of Sciences. 116. 201821936. 10.1073/pnas.1821936116

[93] https://teaching.cornell.edu/teaching-resources/active-collaborative-learning/active-learning

[94] Beichner, Robert & Saul, Jeff & Abbott, David & Morse, Jeanne & Deardorff, Duane & Allain, Rhett & Bonham, Scott & Dancy, Melissa & Risley, John. (2008). Student-centered activities for large enrollment undergraduate programs (SCALE- UP). Research-based Reform of University Physics. 1

[95] THE FUTURES of LEARNING 3: What kind of pedagogies for the 21st century?UNESCO Education Research and Foresight, Paris. [ERF Working Papers Series, No. 15].

[96] Carneiro, R. 2007. The big picture: understanding learning and meta-learning challenges. European Journal of Education, Vol. 42, No. 2, pp. 151-172. http://onlinelibrary.wiley.com/enhanced/doi/10.1111/j.1465-3435.2007.00303.x

[97] Bjork, R. A., & Bjork, E. L. (2020). Desirable difficulties in theory and practice. Journal of Applied research in Memory and Cognition, 9 (4), 475-479.

[98] Harvard Future of Teaching and Learning Task Force -

https://ftltaskforce.harvard.edu/

[99] Al-Hariri MT, Al-Hattami AA. Impact of students' use of technology on their learning achievements in physiology courses at the University of Dammam. J Taibah Univ Med Sci. 2016 Aug 22;12(1):82-85. doi: 10.1016/j.jtumed.2016.07.004. PMID: 31435218; PMCID: PMC6694913.

[100] https://www.harvardmagazine.com/2022/03/harvard-future-teaching-learning-strategies

[101] History of the flipped classroom model and uses of the flipped classroom concept. International Journal of Curriculum and Instructional Studies, 12(1), 71-88. doi: 10.31704/ijocis.2022.004

[102] Abeysekera, L., & Dawson, P. (2015). Motivation and cognitive load in the flipped classroom: Definition, rationale and a call for research. Higher Education Research & Development, 34(1), 1–14. https://doi.org/10.1080/07294360.2014.934336

[103] https://ctl.utexas.edu/instructional-strategies/flipped-classroom

[104] https://www.ncbi.nlm.nih.gov/pmc/articles/PMC7308688/

[105] Nichols, Mark H., Cator, Karen (2008), Challenge Based Learning White Paper. Cupertino, California: Apple, Inc. https://www.apple.com/ca/education/docs/Apple-ChallengedBasedLearning.pdf

[106] Membrillo-Hernández, Jorge & Ramirez, Miguel & Martínez-Acosta, Mariajulia & Cruz-Gómez, Enrique & Muñoz-Díaz, Enrique & Elizalde, Hugo. (2019). Challenge based learning: the importance of world-leading companies as training partners. International Journal on Interactive Design and Manufacturing (IJIDeM). 13. 10.1007/s12008-019-00569-4

[107] https://www.challengebasedlearning.org/2023/08/22/your-brain-on-cbl/

[108] Md Abdullah Al Mamun, Gwendolyn Lawrie, Tony Wright, Instructional design of scaffolded online learning modules for self-directed and inquiry-based learning environments, Computers & Education, Volume 144, 2020, 103695, ISSN 0360-1315, https://doi.org/10.1016/j.compedu.2019.103695.

[109] Schlatter E, Molenaar I, Lazonder AW. Individual Differences in Children's Development of Scientific Reasoning Through Inquiry-Based Instruction: Who Needs Additional Guidance? Front Psychol. 2020 May 14;11:904. doi: 10.3389/fpsyg.2020.00904. PMID: 32477220; PMCID: PMC7241249

[110] Ton de Jong, Ard W. Lazonder, Clark A. Chinn, Frank Fischer, Janice Gobert, Cindy E. Hmelo-Silver, Ken R. Koedinger, Joseph S. Krajcik, Eleni A. Kyza, Marcia C. Linn, Margus Pedaste, Katharina Scheiter, Zacharias C. Zacharia, Let's talk evidence – The case for combining inquiry-based and direct instruction,Educational Research Review, Volume 39, 2023, 100536, ISSN 1747-938X, https://doi.org/10.1016/j.edurev.2023.100536

[111] Why Knowledge Matters: Rescuing Our Children from Failed Educational Theories. E. D. Hirsch, Harvard Education Press, 2016

[112] ibid

[113] Alfieri, L., Brooks, P. J., Aldrich, N. J., & Tenenbaum, H. R. (2011). Does discovery-based instruction enhance learning? Journal of Educational Psychology, 103(1), 1–18. https://doi.org/10.1037/a0021017

[114] BARROWS, H.S. (1986), A taxonomy of problem-based learning methods. Medical Education, 20: 481-486. https://doi.org/10.1111/j.1365-2923.1986.tb01386.x

[115] My Pedagogic Creed by John Dewey. First published in The School Journal, Volume LIV, Number 3 (January 16, 1897), pages 77-80.

[116] Nilson, L. B. (2010). Teaching at its best: A research-based resource for college instructors (2nd ed.). SanFrancisco, CA: Jossey-Bass

[117] Hopper M.K. (2018). Alphabet Soup of Active Learning: Comparison of PBL, CBL, and TBL. HAPS Educator 22 (2): 144-149. doi: 10.21692/haps.2018.019

[118] https://kappanonline.org/research-project-based-learning-de-vivo/

[119] https://kappanonline.org/project-based-learning-ap-advanced-placement-research-saavedra/

[120] Vygotsky, L. S. (1978). Mind in society: The development of higher psychological processes. Massachusetts: Harvard University

Press.

[121] https://www.bbc.com/news/world-asia-49608459

[122] Sitzmann T. (2011). A meta-analytic examination of the instructional effectiveness of computer-based simulation games. Personnel Psychology, 64, 489–528

[123] Paniagua, A. and D. Istance (2018), Teachers as Designers of Learning Environments: The Importance of Innovative Pedagogies, Educational Research and Innovation, OECD Publishing, Paris http://dx.doi.org/10.1787/9789264085374-en

[124] OECD (2018), Teaching for the Future: Effective Classroom Practices To Transform Education, OECD Publishing, Paris, https://doi.org/10.1787/9789264293243-en

[125] Clark, D. B., Tanner-Smith, E. E., & Killingsworth, S. S. (2016). Digital Games, Design, and Learning: A Systematic Review and Meta-Analysis. Review of Educational Research, 86(1), 79-122. https://doi.org/10.3102/0034654315582065

[126] Vogel, J. J., Vogel, D. S., Cannon-Bowers, J., Bowers, C. A., Muse, K., & Wright, M. (2006). Computer gaming and interactive simulations for learning: A meta-analysis. Journal of Educational Computing Research, 34(3), 229–243. https://doi.org/10.2190/FLHV-K4WA-WPVQ-H0YM

[127] Tulloch, R. (2014), "Reconceptualising gamification: Play and pedagogy", Digital Culture & Education, Vol. 6/4, pp. 317-333

[128] Paniagua, A. and D. Istance (2018), Teachers as Designers of Learning Environments: The Importance of Innovative Pedagogies, Educational Research and Innovation, OECD Publishing, Paris

[129] Advances in Physiology Education • doi:10.1152/advan.00001.2019 • http://advan.physiology.org

[130] Veenman, M.V.J.. (2008). Giftedness: Predicting the speed of expertise acquisition by intellectual ability and metacognitive skillfulness of novices. Meta-Cognition: A Recent Review of Research, Theory and Perspectives. 207-220.

[131] Unlock Your Learning, David Kerrigan, 2021. Kindle Direct Publishing

[132] https://www.edutopia.org/article/fostering-metacognition-boost-learning

[133] Nelson, T. O., & Dunlosky, J. (1991). When people's judgments of learning (JOL) are extremely accurate at predicting subsequent recall: The delayed-JOL effect. Psychological Science, 2, 267-270

[134] Hart, J. T. (1965). "Memory and the feeling-of-knowing experience". Journal of Educational Psychology. 56 (4): 208–216. doi:10.1037/h0022263. PMID 5825050

[135] Ericsson, K. A., Krampe, R. T., and Tesch-Römer, C. (1993). The role of deliberate practice in the acquisition of expert performance. Psychol. Rev. 100, 363–406. doi: 10.1037/0033-295X.87.3.215

[136] THE FUTURES of LEARNING 3: What kind of pedagogies for the 21st century?UNESCO Education Research and Foresight, Paris. [ERF Working Papers Series, No. 15]

[137] Ingrid Helleve, Aslaug Grov Almås, "Teachers' Experiences with Networked Classrooms in Norway", Education Research International, vol. 2017, Article ID 8560171, 9 pages, 2017. https://doi.org/10.1155/2017/8560171

[138] OECD (2018), Teaching for the Future: Effective Classroom Practices To Transform Education, OECD Publishing, Paris, https://doi.org/10.1787/9789264293243-en

[139] ibid

[140] Klieme, Eckhard & Pauli, Christine & Reusser, Kurt. (2009). The Pythagoras Study. Investigating effects of teaching and learning in Swiss and German mathematics classrooms. The Power of Video Studies in Investigating Teaching and Learning in the Classroom.

[141] https://teaching.cornell.edu/fall-2020-course-preparation/engaging-students/instructor-presence-and-interaction

[142] Cornelius-White, J. (2007). Learner-centered teacher student relationships are effective: A meta-analysis. Review of Educational Research, 77(1), 113–143

[143] Cynthia Luna Scott. THE FUTURES of LEARNING 3: What kind of pedagogies for the 21st century? UNESCO Education Research and Foresight, Paris. [ERF Working Papers Series, No. 15]

[144] Tawil, S. (2013). Education for "Global Citizenship": A Framework for Discussion. UNESCO Education Research and Foresight (ERF) Working Papers Series 7, Paris: UNESCO

[145] https://www.cast.org/about/about-cast

[146] https://www.vision2030.gov.sa/media/rc0b5oy1/saudi_vision203.pdf

[147] https://www.mckinsey.com/industries/public-sector/our-insights/defining-the-skills-citizens-will-need-in-the-future-world-of-work

[148] https://www.weforum.org/agenda/2023/09/higher-education-model-for-ai/

[149] https://www3.weforum.org/docs/WEF_Future_of_Jobs_2023.pdf

[150] Campos E, Hidrogo I and Zavala G (2022) Impact of virtual reality use on the teaching and learning of vectors. Front. Educ. 7:965640. doi: 10.3389/feduc.2022.965640

[151] https://www.uploadvr.com/sony-prototype-adaptable-haptic-vr-controller/

[152] Entertainment, engagement, and education: Foundations and developments in digital and physical spaces to support learning through making. Giannakos, Michail; Divitini, Monica; Ole Sejer, Iversen. http://hdl.handle.net/11250/2496872. Entertainment Computing. 2017, 21 77-81. 10.1016/j.entcom.2017.04.002

[153] Papert, S. (1991). Situating Constructionism. In I. Harel, & S. Papert (Eds.), Constructionism: Research reports and essays (pp. 1-11). Norwood, NJ: Ablex

[154] Holograms as Teaching Agents, Robin A Walker 2013 J. Phys.: Conf. Ser. 415 012076

[155] https://blog.google/technology/research/project-starline-prototype/

[156] ibid

Made in the USA
Las Vegas, NV
07 November 2023